The Ultimate Guide to
Rulerwork Quilting

FROM *Buying Tools* TO *Planning the Quilting* TO *Successful Stitching*

AMANDA MURPHY

stashBOOKS®
an imprint of C&T Publishing

Publisher: Amy Barrett-Daffin

Creative Director: Gailen Runge

Acquisitions Editor: Roxane Cerda

Managing Editor: Liz Aneloski

Editor: Katie Van Amburg

Technical Editor: Del Walker

Cover/Book Designer: April Mostek

Production Coordinator: Zinnia Heinzmann

Production Editor: Alice Mace Nakanishi

Illustrators: Freesia Pearson Blizard and Amanda Murphy

Cover photography by Edward Weiland; book photography by Edward Weiland, unless otherwise noted

Published by Stash Books, an imprint of C&T Publishing, Inc., P.O. Box 1456, Lafayette, CA 94549

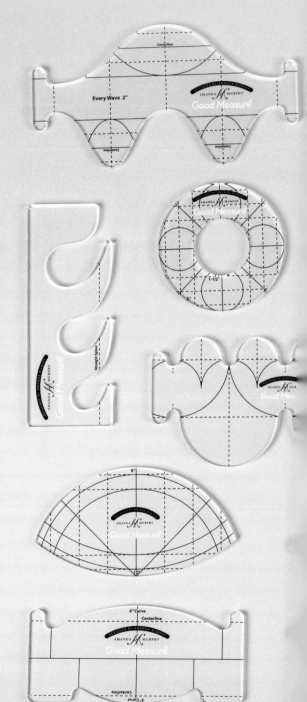

Library of Congress Cataloging-in-Publication Data

Names: Murphy, Amanda, 1971- author.

Title: The ultimate guide to rulerwork quilting : from buying tools to planning the quilting to successful stitching / Amanda Murphy.

Description: Lafayette, CA : Stash Books, an imprint of C&T Publishing, [2020] | Summary: "This companion to Rulerwork Quilting Idea Book provides a technical guide to using quilting rulers with both domestic and longarm machines"-- Provided by publisher.

Identifiers: LCCN 2019043572 | ISBN 9781617459474 (trade paperback) | ISBN 9781617459481 (ebook)

Subjects: LCSH: Machine quilting--Patterns. | Rulers (Instruments)

Classification: LCC TT835 .M8467 2020 | DDC 746.46/041--dc23

LC record available at https://lccn.loc.gov/2019043572

Printed in the USA

10 9 8 7 6 5

Dedication

For my students, who have asked the questions that inspired this book and made me a better teacher in the process. Thank you!—*Amanda*

Acknowledgments

I'd like to extend my gratitude to C&T Publishing for inviting me to design a "how-to" companion for my *Rulerwork Quilting Idea Book* to help people learn to quilt at home. This includes—but is not limited to—Todd Hensley, Amy Barrett-Daffin, Gailen Runge, Liz Aneloski, Katie Van Amburg, Del Walker, April Mostek, Zinnia Heinzmann, Alice Mace Nakanishi, Kelly Burgoyne, Estefany Gonzalez, Rachel Holmes, and Gregory Ligman. Special thanks to my "chief cook and bottle washer" (a.k.a. acquisitions editor) Roxane Cerda, who convinced me at the onset of this project that I definitely could fill 128 pages with how-to-do rulerwork instructions and then patiently listened to me do so out loud over the course of two long days. Also for teaching me what an "amanuensis" is, because I obviously need one. Thanks to our wonderful photographer Edward Weiland of Edward Weiland Photography—this book would not have been possible without him and his patience and attention to detail. (Also, I'm pretty sure he could teach quilting now!) And thank you to the lovely makeup artist, Ashlynn Raquel, who rescued me from my lack of expertise in this area!

And, of course, a very special thanks goes out to BERNINA of America and BERNINA International. I am so fortunate to be an Expert and Quilting and Longarm Spokesperson for this company that leads the industry in innovation. Their machines have provided me with the tools and inspiration to create my art, and their willingness to collaborate has allowed me to develop educational tools to teach others what I've learned in the process. I'm honored to call so many of them friends and mentors.

Thanks also to Benartex Fabrics, who has met the challenge of printing many of my panels designed to teach rulerwork and quilting.

And, last but not least, I'd like to extend my gratitude to Brewer Sewing for inviting me to design a line of rulers incorporating extensive markings and for figuring out how to make them nonskid in the process. Thanks so much to everyone on the Brewer team!

Photo by C&T Publishing

Contents

Introduction

Why rulers?

Well, to answer that, we have to go back to the beginning of quilting itself. Rulers have always been used in piecing to allow us to be precise and to create repeating designs. And, with the advent of rotary cutters, rulers became a must-have tool. Ask any piecer if they could limit themselves to *just one* ruler!

In the age of hand quilting, various methods could be used to mark quilts and we could place stitches precisely along those lines. Have you ever seen a beautifully hand-quilted feather wreath? Usually marked by pouncing chalk through a template, they are exquisite and very uniform. But try to free-motion quilt that on a machine—it isn't so easy, is it? And so, as more machines capable of quilting came onto the market, our visual vocabulary of feathers began to evolve. We came to expect, and even find beautiful, asymmetrical feathers with a wide variety of plume styles. After all, our free-motion feathers are no more varied than nature itself! (*Well, maybe just a little more varied.*)

Then came the advent of longarm quilting machines, which allowed us to move a sewing head along a frame upon which a quilt was mounted. But how to quilt straight lines around the blocks or along the seams? Longarms don't have feed dogs like domestic machines. They can quilt straight lines in a horizontal or vertical direction with channel locks, but many times the seams on our quilts aren't perfectly straight. (At least mine aren't!)

Rulers to the rescue! Thick plastic quilting rulers, sometimes called templates, can be used to quilt straight lines in any direction! And they can be adjusted as you quilt so if your seam is a little wobbly, your stitching will still lie right along it!

Well, it didn't take creative quilters long to realize that they didn't have to settle for just straight-line rulers. There are a ton of other shapes just waiting to be explored....

Quilting, using my Good Measure Every Angle quilting ruler on a BERNINA Q 24 Longarm Quilting Machine

A free-motion quilted feather

Photo by Amanda Murphy

A world of rulers! These are from my line of Good Measure quilting rulers for Brewer Sewing.

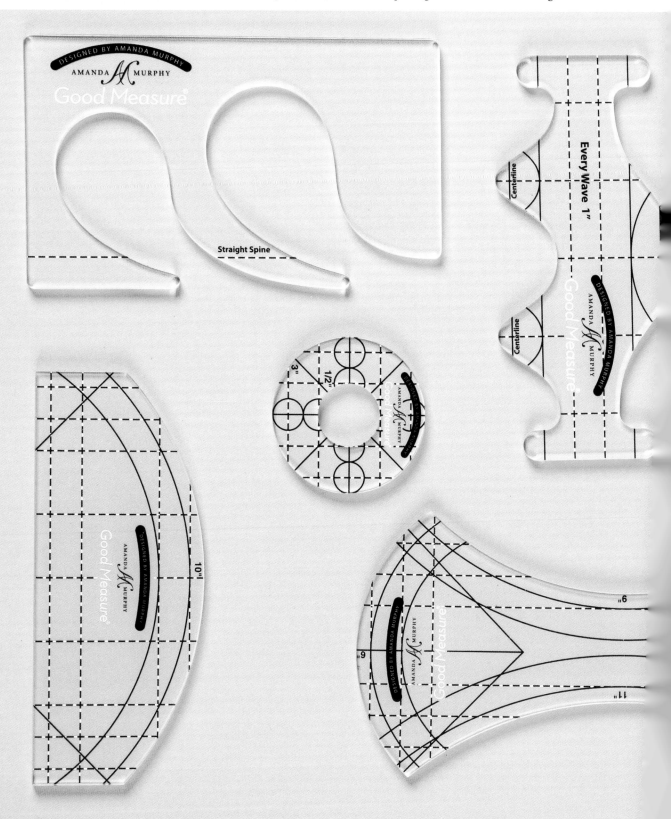

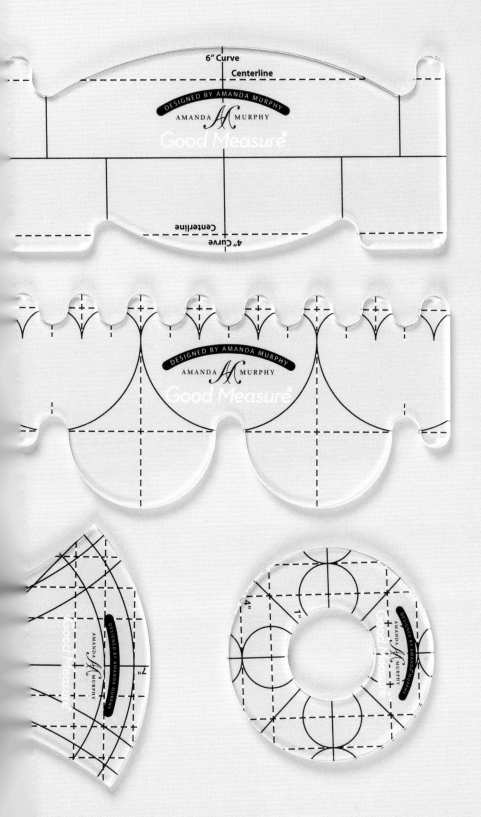

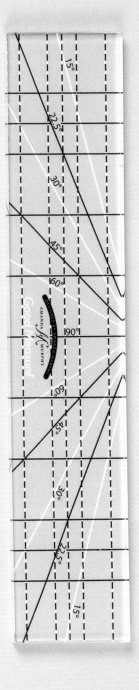

Technology and Art

So, longarm quilters began to create designs with large, dynamic shapes made possible by rulers and, to no one's surprise, once again our quilting aesthetic began to evolve.

As domestic machine quilters began to see these quilts in shows, they wanted in on the fun, and domestic ruler feet were born! The method of quilting is a little different on domestic machines, but the same results can be achieved.

Quilting with rulers on domestic machines has the added benefit of minimizing the need to rotate the quilt under the machine. As

any domestic quilter can attest, that in itself cuts down on a lot of effort and time. Plus, when you quilt with a ruler, you naturally change quilting directions more easily than you would with a walking foot, and quilting in many directions generally ensures a squarer top than quilting in just one. (Quilting parallel lines in just one direction on a quilt can result in a diamond-shape quilt, which is all well and good if that was what you intended, but it can be pretty disappointing if you were going for a square.)

I am lucky enough to teach rulerwork, on both domestic and longarm machines, to hundreds of people across the nation and around the world every year, and I've learned a few things along the way.

Want to see how it is done? Read on. ...

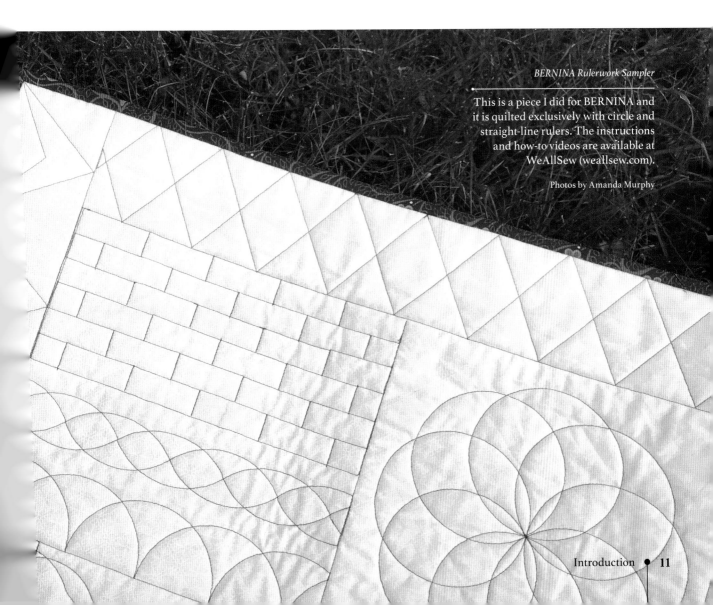

BERNINA Rulerwork Sampler

This is a piece I did for BERNINA and it is quilted exclusively with circle and straight-line rulers. The instructions and how-to videos are available at WeAllSew (weallsew.com).

Photos by Amanda Murphy

Tools

This chapter describes some of the tools you will need in addition to quilting rulers (for more information, see Rulers, page 29).

Machines

Domestic Machines

For rulerwork, choose a machine with free-motion capabilities and excellent stitch quality. I've quilted on both my BERNINA 5 and 7 Series for years, and I highly recommend them. One of the things that I like about BERNINAs is that when you lower the feed dogs, they actually turn off rather than keep running, which minimizes the vibration on the machine bed.

A bigger throat space is hugely advantageous, particularly for larger quilts, but it is not an absolute necessity, especially for smaller projects. Don't let having a small machine discourage you from trying out these techniques. As your skill set broadens, you'll be able to better judge what you can accomplish with the tools you have, and you can do a lot with a little machine and a little creativity!

For domestic quilting, you will be moving the fabric in tandem with the ruler, and the larger the machine bed, the more contact it will have with the fabric and ruler, making the entire assembly easier to move. Of course, you can extend your machine bed by seating it in a cabinet or Sew Steady Table. See more details about this and other modifications you can make in Accessories (page 21).

(page 21).

Note: Choose Your Dealer Carefully
Regardless of what brand of machine you buy, a good dealer network is important. Your dealer is your main contact for any problems or questions about your machine—choose one you trust and are comfortable with!

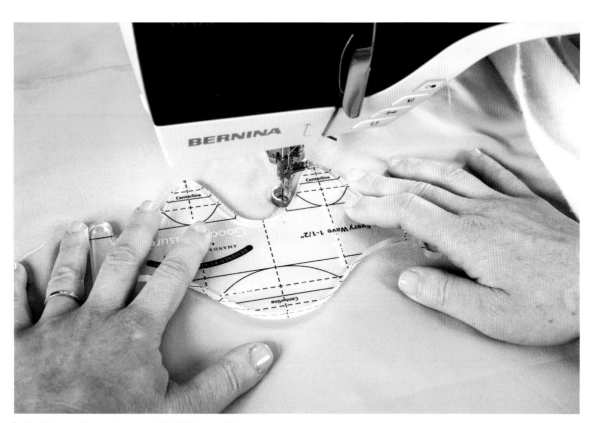

↑ Quilting with a ruler on a BERNINA 790 Plus

Longarm Machines in a Sit-Down Configuration

When I saw the BERNINA Q 20 Sit-Down Longarm Quilting Machine for the first time, it was love at first sight! Well, maybe it was like a first crush until I sewed ... but then I was head over heels in love! This machine is a true longarm and can even be mounted on a frame. It's great for people who like to sit while quilting; it offers a 20″ throat space and unparalleled visibility.

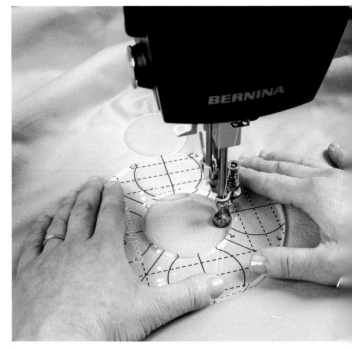

↑ Quilting with a ruler on a BERNINA Q 20

But, perhaps best of all, BERNINA mounted two stitch regulators in the base of this machine so that you have stitch regulation with whatever free-motion foot you choose to use. **News flash:** *This means you have stitch regulation with a ruler foot!* This is truly a game changer—it is *much* easier to do rulerwork with stitch regulation and, since you have to remove the stitch regulator to put on the ruler foot on a BERNINA domestic, that means the Q 20 has superpowers!

↑ The BERNINA stitch regulators peeking up out of the Q 20's machine bed

Longarm and Midarm Machines on Frames

So what are the advantages of longarms as far as rulerwork is concerned? Well, with longarms, you don't have to move the rulers in tandem with the fabric. You simply glide the machine with the foot against the ruler. That means your dominant arm will do much of the work while your non-dominant hand holds the ruler. Because you will probably be stitching with rulers for many hours, it is important to look for a longarm that glides effortlessly over the frame.

If you are planning to do rulerwork, you should look for a longarm with stitch regulation. This is one of the benefits of longarm quilting, as it makes rulerwork *much* easier. I like BERNINA's Stitch Regulation Mode 2 for rulerwork because it allows me to reposition my ruler with the machine running, without creating a knot on the back of the quilt.

There are many longarms and midarms on the market at a wide range of price points, and they can look similar but feel completely different. I like the BERNINA Q 24 Longarm Quilting Machine because of its ease of movement. It also has completely adjustable handlebars, which allow me to change my grip throughout the day as I quilt. *Changing movement is very important with a hobby that places repetitive stress on our body!* Because the buttons on the Q 24 handles are programmable, I'm working on being able to do rulerwork with my nondominant arm; as of this writing I haven't mastered it, but I'm making progress!

Quilting with a ruler on a BERNINA Q 24

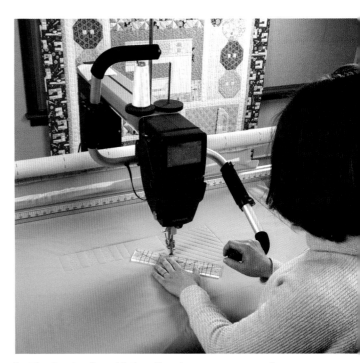

The Q 24's adjustable handles give great access to the quilting area, allowing me to hold rulers in place easily. You can even program the buttons!

You'll want to look for a longarm that can be equipped with a ruler foot and ruler table. The ruler table will give you a stable surface under the quilt top on which to rest the rulers. I'll talk more about feet in Ruler Feet (page 18), but note that *the ability to move the ruler foot up and down is a huge plus*. Look for this while shopping because some long arms on the market don't allow you to move the foot up or down at all. One of the things that I like about the BERNINA Q 24 is that you can raise and lower the ruler foot automatically right from the screen or from the handlebars. You can also control thread tension digitally on screen!

↑ On the Q 24, I like to do rulerwork in BSR2 mode, so it keeps my stitches the same length without making knots on the back of the piece. The Q 24's interface allows you to raise and lower the foot onscreen …

↓ … or on the handles!

A dead bar on the back of a longarm is a must for custom work in my opinion, as it allows me to work up and down the quilt, building my quilting density gradually, keeping my top square. (For my process, see Planning a Quilt with Rulers, page 71.)

↑ The dead bar keeps your quilt level as you work!

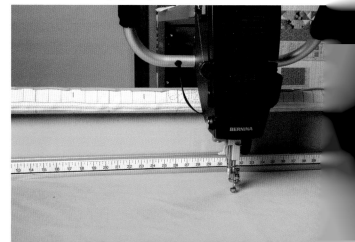

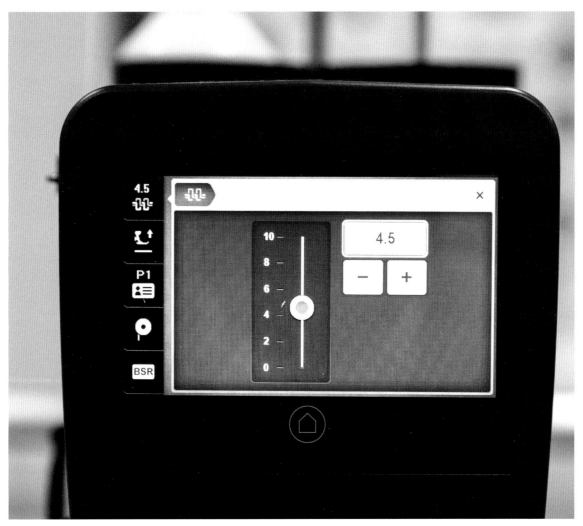

⬆ You can also adjust thread tension digitally!

I also appreciate that the Q 24 takes domestic sewing machine needles, which, unlike standard longarm needles, have a flat back for easy insertion. Plus, I can use any of my BERNINA free-motion feet with or without stitch regulation.

Note
As a BERNINA Expert, I'm very familiar with the machines in the BERNINA line, so this is what is shown here. There are obviously a lot of other machines on the market, too. If you have questions about any of them and their suitability for rulerwork, please consult your local dealer.

Ruler Feet

So, what is so special about a ruler foot? Well, I'm glad you asked! The feature that defines a ruler foot is its high profile. This profile allows you to glide the foot right along the edge of the ruler. If you didn't have it, the ruler could potentially slip right into the path of your needle. *Never ever* try rulerwork without a ruler foot mounted on your machine.

The type of ruler foot determines the ruler thickness that you can use, so it is very important to know which type of foot works with your machine! There are several different types of rulers out there, and I've met dozens of people who have invested in ruler sets only to find that they were the wrong thickness for their ruler foot.

Note
Plastic tolerances aren't as precise as metal tolerances, so you might find some slight variation in ruler thickness.

For Longarms

Remember how rulers were originally developed for longarms? Longarms are "hopping foot" machines. While they stitch, the foot actually moves up and down just a bit, so you need thick rulers to accommodate that movement—otherwise, the ruler could slip under the foot. For that reason, "longarm thickness rulers" are approximately ¼″ or 6 mm thick. *All longarm ruler feet are meant to be used with rulers that are that thickness.*

The BERNINA Ruler Foot #96 was developed specially for the BERNINA Q Series machines. Note the high profile of the sole.

Photo by BERNINA International

For Domestics and *Longarms*

BERNINA has developed the Adjustable Ruler Foot #72, a ruler foot especially for use with all the domestic BERNINA machines manufactured in the past few decades.

The BERNINA Adjustable Ruler Foot #72 was developed for domestic BERNINA machines, but can also be used on their Q Series. | Photo by BERNINA International

THIS FOOT HAS SEVERAL UNIQUE FEATURES:

- It mounts high up in the machine, giving you a deep curve down into the sole of the foot that allows true "longarm thickness" rulers to fit all the way around the sole's perimeter. You can also use high-shank or low-shank rulers when this foot is mounted on a domestic machine because it will not hop, but in general, thinner rulers are more difficult to control.

- Its gold dial allows you to raise and lower the foot to the surface of the fabric easily. So if you have an especially thick seam you need to quilt across there is no need to get out a screwdriver!

- Most importantly, *it incorporates a spring!* Normally, there is the potential for the needle bar to collide with the profile of a ruler foot on a domestic machine if you forget to put the foot down before putting the needle down. This spring prevents that from happening. This spring is so important that, although you can use the #72 foot on the BERNINA longarm, you would not want to use the #96 foot on a domestic because of the absence of the spring!

So I highly recommend purchasing a #72 foot if you own a compatible BERNINA. (Note that the use of third-party feet on BERNINAs voids their warranty.)

Longarm thickness rulers can fit all the way around the BERNINA Adjustable Ruler Foot #72.

The gold dial allows you to raise and lower the foot to the machine bed.

What If You Don't Own a BERNINA?

Ask your dealer about a ruler foot that will work on your machine. More and more machine companies are likely to develop feet specific to their models, and if a ruler foot developed for your machine becomes available from the manufacturer, I recommend its purchase.

If a manufacturer foot is not available, Westalee Design makes a number of feet that can be used on many brands. Your dealer should be able to help you figure out which would be best for yours.

Since these feet do not have springs, you'll want to be sure you *always* lower the foot before lowering the needle when quilting.

High-shank feet are designed to take rulers 4.5 mm thick or less. Low-shank feet can only take rulers that are around 3.0 mm thick. There just isn't a lot of room behind a low-shank foot to fit a ruler. Low-shank rulers can be a little harder to control than their thicker counterparts.

Never ever use cutting rulers to do rulerwork— they are too thin!

A Longarm- Thickness Ruler and a High-Shank Foot?

Sometimes, depending on how your foot mounts on your machine, you can get away with using a longarm-thickness ruler with a high-shank foot. You'll be able to do this if you can move the ruler all the way around the perimeter of the sole when the foot is down. But test this before you buy a bunch of rulers you can't use!

A Westalee high- and low-shank foot. Note that the areas behind these feet are more compressed than that of a longarm foot, and the machine's foot mount can sometimes extend into the foot area. This means you'll need to use thinner rulers than you would use on a longarm.

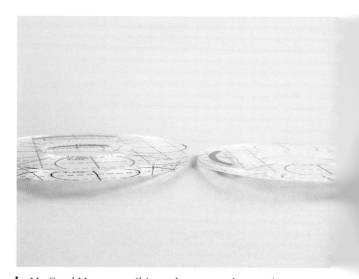

My Good Measure quilting rulers currently come in "longarm" and "low-shank" thicknesses.

Accessories

Sewing Cabinets and Tables
(Domestic Machines Only)

Most tables that come with sewing machines are not completely flat because they are designed for garment sewing. For rulerwork, this means that some part of the ruler might actually be hanging off the flat portion of the table, which isn't ideal. (To see the disaster that happens where you hold a ruler on the curved edge of a sewing table, refer to the photo, page 108!) The greater the surface area of the ruler that has contact with the flat portion of the table, the easier it is to control the quilting.

Sewing cabinets, in which the machine sits so that its bed is flat to the cabinet's top surface, are ideal.

If that isn't a possibility, Sew Steady makes quilting tables for many machines that provide you with an extended flat quilting area.

Supreme Sliders or Free-Motion Gliders
(Domestic Machines Only)

To make moving your quilt sandwich easier, I highly recommend a Free Motion Glider (by Sew Steady) or a Supreme Slider (by LaPierre Studio). These can be affixed to the top of the machine bed to help the quilt glide easily more easily over the surface.

One note: If the underside of either of these products becomes dusty, it will not adhere to the bed of the machine. For this reason, it is always good to store these products inside their original packaging. If they do become dusty, you can clean them with a wipe and let them dry before adhering them to the machine bed.

The RMF MULTI sewing table offers two electronically controlled height adjustments—both the height of the table and the height of the machine can be adjusted! A table like this is ideal for rulerwork. | Photo by RMF

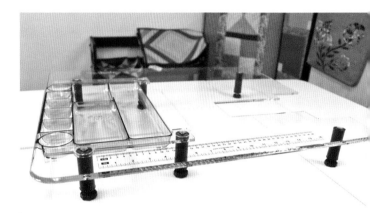

Sew Steady Wish Table | Photo by Sew Steady

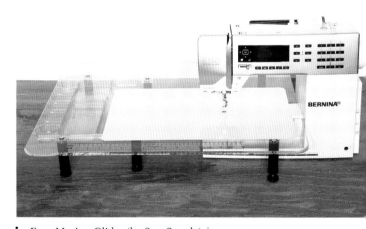

Free-Motion Glider (by Sew Steady) | Photo by C&T Publishing

Quilting Gloves (Domestic Machines Only)

I always use quilting gloves when free-motion quilting on a domestic machine, but also frequently just keep them on for rulerwork, since I switch back and forth between the two techniques all the time. There are many great styles of gloves on the market. They are optional when you are using rulers, but if you have better results using them, go for it!

Needles

When quilting, you need to choose a needle with a sharp point. Jeans, topstitch, sharps, and embroidery needles are all candidates. I usually choose size 80/12 or 90/14 jeans or topstitch needles for my work on both the BERNINA longarm and BERNINA domestics when I'm using 40- and 50-weight Aurifil cotton thread respectively, because I like the bigger eye relative to the needle's shaft. Remember, the correct needle size depends on the type, brand, and weight of thread you are using.

Many brands of longarms require industrial needles. Consult your manual for details.

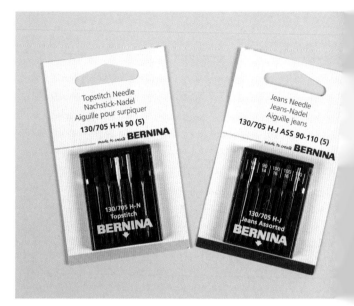

↑ Some of my preferred needles for quilting

Thread

There are many different great threads on the market. Keep in mind that the threads need to be strong because of the long thread path and stitching speed. My favorite is the Aurifil cotton in both 50- and 40-weights, but there are also many great polyester and specialty options out there. For extrafine work, I love the look of kimono silk. (I would use a size 70 needle for silk.)

I generally match my bobbin and top threads, unless I'm using a specialty thread like a monofilament or metallic. In those cases, I follow the manufacturer's recommendation.

↑ Some of my favorite threads | Photo by C&T Publishing

Cleaning Brush and Oil

Cleaning your machine is so important! There is so much needle movement in quilting that, even with the finest of threads, there can be lint buildup. Make sure you brush out your machine with each use and *never* blow canned air into the interior.

Not all machines require oil, but if you own a BERNINA, you know BERNINAs *love* oil—that is because they have metal parts (which is a good thing!). After a few hours of stitching, you will probably begin to notice a "dull" sound. This often means your machine is thirsty, so give it a drink—it has been working hard. (BERNINA longarms like their oil too!)

I clean and oil first thing every morning I quilt. If I'm quilting throughout the day I will frequently oil a second time and clean a few extra times. Be sure *not* to oil at the end of the day. The machine's movement distributes the oil, so if you oil and then walk away, that oil will just drip down to the bottom of the machine.

If you have any questions about cleaning or the need to oil, consult your dealer.

Don't forget to get your machine serviced annually (or even semi-annually if you quilt a lot!) to keep it in good working order. Your technician can get into places you can't and make sure your machine is in tip-top condition!

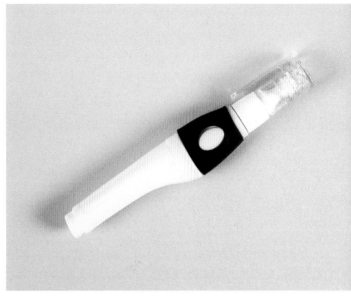

My trusty BERNINA oil pen

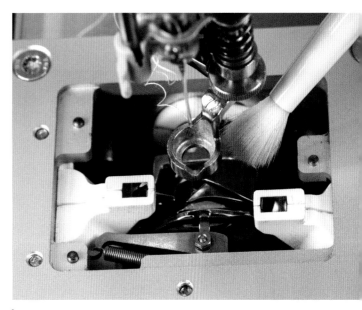

I like to clean with a big, soft brush I picked up at a chain store. I have lots of them hanging around my studio so that I never have to go looking for one.

Quilt Clips (Longarms Only)

Quilt Clips (by The Grace Company) attach to the front of your frame and help control the quilt top as you quilt. They are particularly helpful for controlling the top when you opt to have your quilt "float" unsecured instead of pinning the bottom of it to a front rail to keep it square.

↑ Quilt Clips (by The Grace Company)

Ruler Tape

Many rulers on the market today can be a bit slippery. Putting some tape onto the side that has contact with the fabric (which is the side with the printing or the etched lines) can really help. It can be anything as simple as little rings of painter's tape, like you are wrapping a present, to tape made specifically for this purpose.

One caveat: Some rougher tapes made specifically for longarm machines can scratch a sewing cabinet or table if you aren't really careful. I prefer Westalee Design's Stable Tape for use with domestic machines because it is soft and won't scratch anything!

Note: No Tape Necessary!
My Good Measure quilting rulers for Brewer Sewing have a nonskid backing, so there is no need for tape!

↑ Backing a ruler with painter's tape can work in a pinch!

Stable Tape from Westalee Design (by Sew Steady)—a good solution for all quilting scenarios!
Photo by C&T Publishing

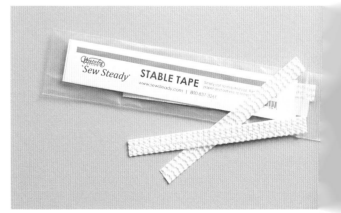

Echoing Tools

You can extend the versatility of your rulers with echo clips. The ones shown here are made by BERNINA to fit around their Adjustable Ruler Foot #72. They add distance between the needle and the edge of the ruler, giving you additional shapes with which to work. For instance, if you have a ruler that quilts a 6″ circle, you can use the echo clips and the same ruler to produce circles that are 6½″, 7″, and 7½″!

Westalee Design makes similar products called Echo Guides that are available for all their ruler feet.

BERNINA Echo Clips

Using a BERNINA Echo Clip to quilt a 3½″ circle with a ruler that would normally quilt a 3″ circle

Marking Tools

Marking tools are a must. I prefer to use a white chalk wheel liner marker (such as Chaco Liner) or a Hera Marker, which just creases the fabric; but when I can't, I sometimes use a blue water-soluble marking pen. I recommend washing the marks out as soon as possible because if you forget and hit the blue marks with an iron, they become permanent. (Ask me how I know!)

Westalee Design's crosshair square ruler can be a time-saver for marking blocks for rulerwork because it allows you to delineate 16 equal quadrants around a central point in seconds.

I also keep painter's tape and a fine-tip permanent marker on hand in case I want to make additional markings on my rulers. I always mark on the side that won't be in contact with the quilt, just to be safe. (That is the side *without* the printed or etched lines.) Marks can be removed from rulers with rubbing alcohol.

Batting

Use a high-quality batting from your local quilt shop. Not all battings are the same. I tend to like natural fibers, such as cotton, bamboo, or wool. For added loft, you can layer wool on top of cotton. I also love Quilters Dream Orient for really special quilts.

I don't usually recommend polyester for bed quilts, but for wall quilts, a bit of polyester can help keep the batting from drifting downward over time.

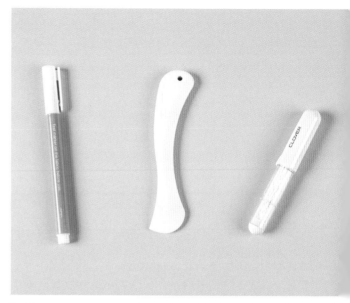

↑ Chaco Liner, Hera Marker, and water-soluble pen

↑ 8 Point Crosshair Ruler from Westalee Design (by Sew Steady) | Photo by C&T Publishing

Ruler Panels

One of the things I'm proudest of in my work in this industry is pioneering the use of panels to teach rulerwork. I started by designing a ruler panel for BERNINA, and over time I've added, and will continue to add, more panels to the mix. I also create ruler guides with lots of diagrams that show you how to use the panels. The rulers coordinate with fabric collections and are printed beautifully by Benartex.

I hope they inspire you to use rulers to create designs on your own!

Photos by Amanda Murphy

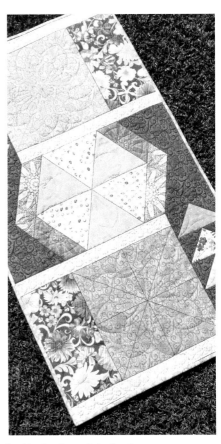

BERNINA Ruler Panel

This original *BERNINA Ruler Panel* was designed to be used with the original BERNINA ruler sets.

Jubilee Gold Ruler Panel

The *Jubilee Gold Ruler Panel*, designed to commemorate BERNINA's 125th anniversary and which uses my BERNINA Jubilee Rulers, was created to coordinate with the *BERNINA 125th Anniversary Quilt* (page 101).

Meadow Dance Ruler Panel

The *Meadow Dance Ruler Panel* was created to coordinate with specific Westalee ruler sets.

Jubilee Holiday Ruler Panel pillows

These pillows were made from the Jubilee Holiday Ruler Panel, also with the BERNINA Jubilee Ruler Set.

Photos by C&T Publishing

Area 5: Horizontal Diamonds & Petals

Every Oval 2" × 4" (inside)

This time we'll quilt the same design as we did in Area 3, with a little twist. Instead of orienting the ruler vertically, we'll turn it into a horizontal position suitable for narrow and long areas like sashing.

When you are quilting on the bottom edge of the quilting area the centerline on the ruler should align with the points on the panel.

Complete the bottom scallops. Free-motion up the side of the quilting area to start the top scallops.

When you are quilting on the top edge of the quilting area the centerline on the ruler should align with the top edge of the quilting area.

Starting in the bottom left corner use the edge of ruler to quilt up to the alignment point.

Shift the ruler over to the other side of the foot and quilt back down to the bottom of the quilting area.

Continue across until you get to the right side of the quilting area. Free-motion or use a straight line ruler to quilt up the right side of the quilting area.

Quilt back to the left, making a second pass offset from the first.

Area 6: Cathedral Windows

Every Oval 5" × 10" (outside)

This is a variation of scallops that is easy with oval rulers! The centerline of the Every Oval 5" × 10" ruler will always be aligned with the bottom of the quilting area, but unlike scallops, you will not quilt all the way round the top of the ruler.

A page from my Celestial Lights Ruler Panel Guide

Detail of *Celestial Lights Ruler Panel* (full quilt, page 82)

This panel uses my new Good Measure Every Oval quilting rulers for Brewer Sewing.

Photo by Amanda Murphy

Rulers

This section will introduce some ruler shapes on the market today to use with the machines, ruler feet, and other tools (see Tools, page 12). If you have a ruler and a quilt sandwich in hand and can't wait to jump right in, skip to Planning a Quilt with Rulers (page 71) and then come back to this section when you are ready to see more!

Students ask me all the time, "What rulers should I buy?" The correct answer is the rulers that you will use the most, and that depends upon the style of quilt you like to make.

Note

Note that all the photos in this section are shot on a longarm machine. For more detailed photos of the process of quilting on a longarm, see Executing Rulerwork on a Longarm Machine (page 117). For details on how to work with rulers on a domestic machine, see Executing Rulerwork on a Domestic Machine (page 102).

Ruler Thickness Cheat Sheet

Wondering what thickness of rulers you should buy? Here's a handy cheat sheet!

Scenario 1

You own a longarm on a frame and only intend to quilt on that.

- *Solution:* Buy only "longarm thickness" rulers, or rulers that are approximately ¼˝ or 6mm.

Scenario 2

You own a Sit-Down longarm (such as the BERNINA Q 20) in a table, and you only intend to quilt on it.

- *Solution:* Buy only "longarm thickness" rulers—rulers that are approximately ¼˝ or 6mm.

Scenario 3

You quilt on a domestic BERNINA equipped with the Adjustable Ruler Foot #72. You don't own another brand of machine that you intend to use for quilting.

- *Solution:* Buy longarm rulers so that, should you ever invest in a Q 20 or Q 24 or any longarm, you'll still be able to use your rulers!

Scenario 4

You own a machine that you'd like to use for quilting, and it uses a high-shank ruler foot.

- *Solution:* Buy high-shank rulers. (You can *occasionally* fit a longarm ruler behind high-shank feet on some machines, but not always. See A Longarm-Thickness Ruler and a High-Shank Foot?, page 20.)

Scenario 5

You own a machine that you'd like to use for quilting, and it uses a low-shank ruler foot.

- *Solution:* Buy low-shank rulers.

Scenario 6

You own a machine that you'd like to use for quilting and it uses either a high-shank or low-shank ruler foot, but you also have a longarm or a sit-down style longarm and you would like to quilt with it, too.

- *Solution:* Sadly, the solution is to choose between the machines or buy two sets of rulers.

Basic Rulers

In general, I think that you can never go wrong with basic shapes. A straight-line ruler and a set of circles will give you a lot of design possibilities. In fact, over half the designs in my *Rulerwork Quilting Idea Book* are based on these two shapes alone!

My Good Measure quilting rulers for Brewer Sewing feature a generous surface area and a special nonslip backing, so there is no need for tape! But it is their clear and copious markings that have made them a favorite among quilters. When designing these rulers, I put on the marks that I have always wanted, and I hope you find them useful as well.

They currently come in two thicknesses—longarm and shank.

The measurements indicated on my Good Measure quilting rulers refer to the quilted size or the shape, rather than the ruler size. There are a lot of extra markings, too, which greatly simplify the quilting process and minimize the need to mark the quilt top!

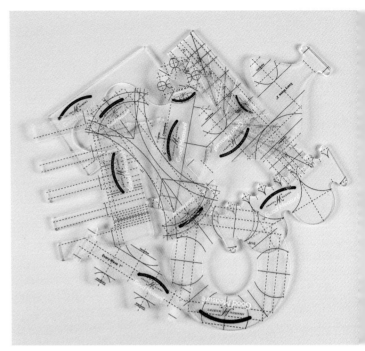

There are so many shapes of rulers available, it can be confusing to know which to explore first.

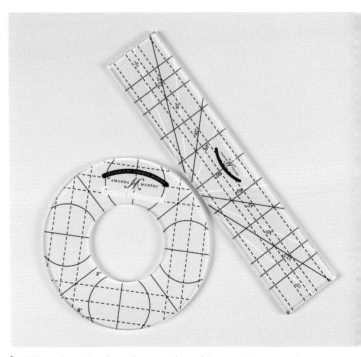

When shopping for rulers, good markings are important! There are a lot of markings on my Good Measure quilting rulers because Brewer Sewing let me have free rein. Thanks, Brewer!

You can use the tips in this book with any set of quilting rulers, so raid your ruler stash for similar shapes and meet me back here to learn how to use them! Once you have learned the basic technique, consult my *Rulerwork Quilting Idea Book* for an expansive library of design ideas.

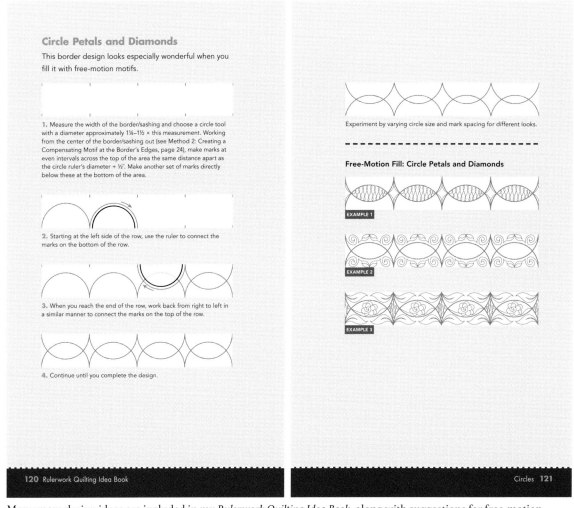

Circle Petals and Diamonds

This border design looks especially wonderful when you fill it with free-motion motifs.

1. Measure the width of the border/sashing and choose a circle tool with a diameter approximately 1¼–1½ × this measurement. Working from the center of the border/sashing out (see Method 2: Creating a Compensating Motif at the Border's Edges, page 24), make marks at even intervals across the top of the area the same distance apart as the circle ruler's diameter + ½˝. Make another set of marks directly below these at the bottom of the area.

2. Starting at the left side of the row, use the ruler to connect the marks on the bottom of the row.

3. When you reach the end of the row, work back from right to left in a similar manner to connect the marks on the top of the row.

4. Continue until you complete the design.

Experiment by varying circle size and mark spacing for different looks.

Free-Motion Fill: Circle Petals and Diamonds

EXAMPLE 1

EXAMPLE 2

EXAMPLE 3

Many more design ideas are included in my *Rulerwork Quilting Idea Book*, along with suggestions for free-motion motifs to enhance your rulerwork! | Photo by C&T Publishing

Recommended Good Measure quilting ruler set: **EVERY ANGLE**

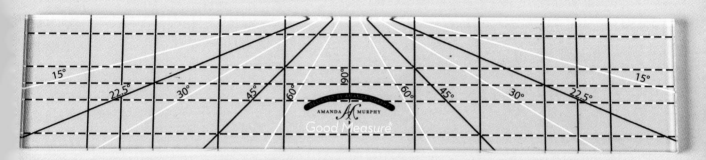

↑ My Good Measure Every Angle ruler

Straight-line rulers are usually the simplest for people to use because the motion is similar to that of regular piecing. Remember, your stitched line will always be ¼″ from the edge of the ruler—another similarity to piecing. (Thank goodness it is a ¼″—I don't think I could eyeball anything else as well!)

Here are some of my favorite straight-line designs:

PIANO KEYS

Piano keys are a quick and easy way to
fill a border, and they look particularly
great when contrasted with free-motion.

Quilt the border edges or the edges of the
quilting area before beginning the keys. You'll
travel up the side of these previously quilted lines
to get from row to row.

Use the perpendicular lines on the ruler to help aid
you in knowing how far to travel along the edge of
the quilting area before you begin the first piano key.
(The lines on my Good Measure rulers are always ¼″,
½″, or 1″ apart. If you don't have perpendicular lines
on your ruler, you can apply some painter's tape at
strategic intervals.) Here, I am using the lines on the
ruler to make sure that the piano keys are 1″ apart.

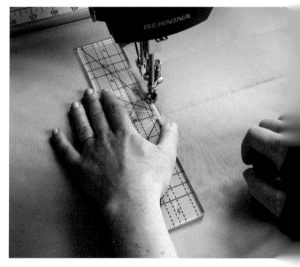

Turn the ruler to begin the first piano key. One
of the lines on the ruler should lie right on top
of the previously stitched line. Here, the line
I've chosen to use is ¾″ away from the ruler's
edge. When you add it to the ¼″ distance from
the needle to the edge of the ruler stitch, that
means the piano keys will be 1″ wide. Quilt
across the quilting area.

Use the perpendicular lines on the ruler to travel 1″ along the side of the quilting area ...

... and quilt the next piano key.

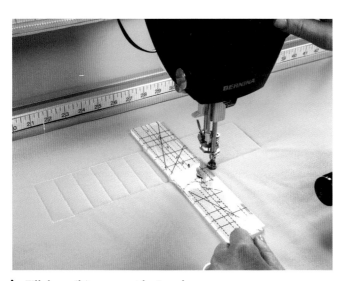

Fill the quilting area with piano keys.

If desired, go back and fill every other piano key with a free-motion fill—that will make some of the piano keys appear puffy!

CROSSHATCHING

Crosshatching is a great background fill.
I particularly love it behind appliqué. Be on
the lookout for diamond prints to make quilting this pattern even easier!

Quilt in- (or along-) the-ditch around the
quilting area. For a traditional crosshatch
design, use the lines on your ruler to establish
a 45° line through the quilting area. (If you
don't have angle lines on your quilting ruler,
you might have to mark the angle with your
cutting ruler first.)

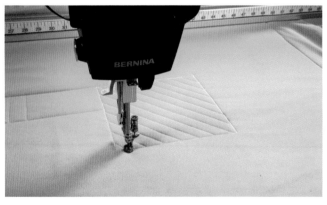

Fill the quilting area with lines that are parallel and at
equal intervals to the first.

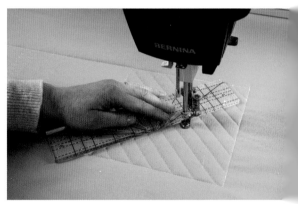

Use the ruler to establish a line at a 90° angle
to the first set of lines.

Fill the quilting area with lines that are parallel and at
equal intervals.

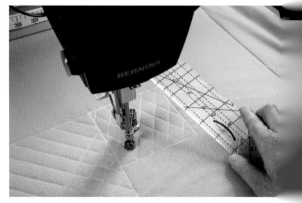

To quilt a diamond crosshatch, do exactly the
same thing, but vary the angle of the lines,
using the angled lines on your ruler. This is
a diamond pattern, using the 60° lines on the
Every Angle Ruler.

SUNBURSTS

Rays are one of my favorite motifs because they add direction and movement to a quilt top. See *Diamond Jubilee* (page 79) and *Amethyst Jubilee* (page 80) for good examples of this!

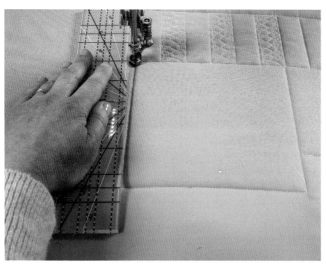

Quilt in- (or along-) the-ditch around the quilting area. Then, starting in a corner, snug up your ruler and angle it in from the edge of the quilting area, until the edge of the ruler is right on top of the edge of the quilting area.

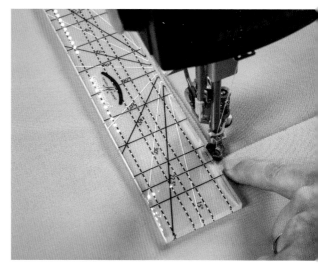

Quilt along the ruler, stopping when the edge of the foot hits the edge of the quilting area.

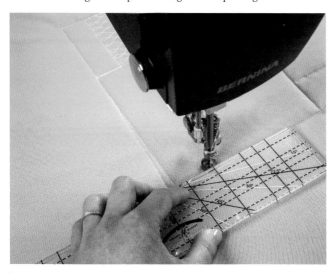

Quilt a little up the edge of the block.

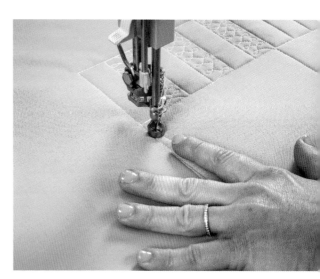

Stitch back down toward the original corner, but stop just short of it. (Not quilting into the corner each time will minimize thread buildup.)

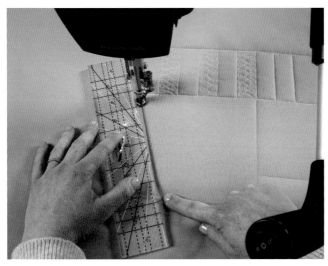

Turn the ruler again so that the edge of the ruler is right on top of the edge of the previous ray.

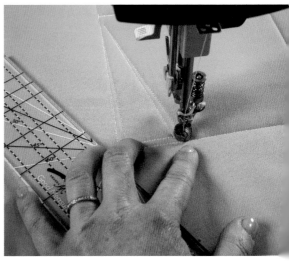

Quilt along the rulers, stopping when the edge of the foot hits the edge of the quilting area.

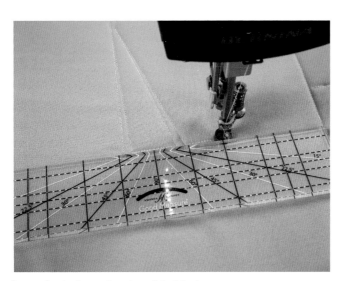

Quilt a little up the edge of the block.

Continue making rays until you've filled the quilting area. On the last ray, quilt back down into the corner.

Circles

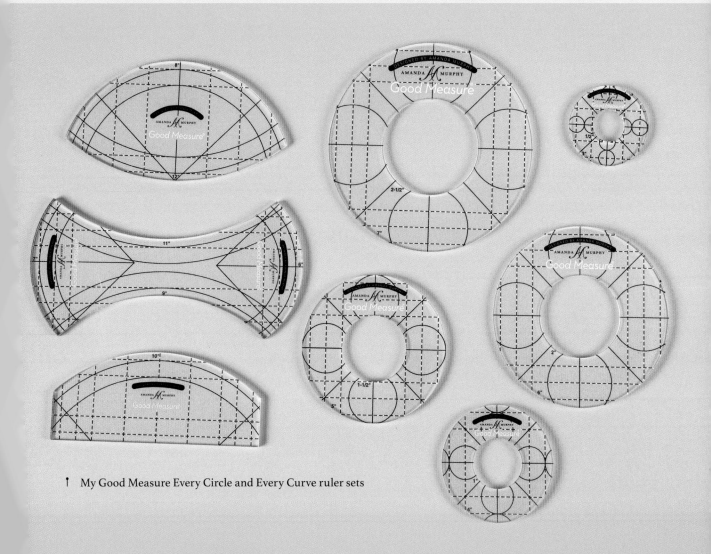

↑ My Good Measure Every Circle and Every Curve ruler sets

When working with circles, you should be most concerned with the size and shape of the quilted curve, rather than that of the plastic itself. Because of this, the measurements indicated on my Good Measure quilting ruler sets refer to the quilted curves.

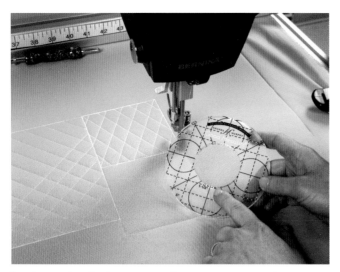

This circle ruler from my Good Measure Every Circle set quilts a 5″ circle if you quilt around the outside of the ruler. This means the ruler itself measures 4½″ from edge to edge. If you stitch around the inside of the ruler, it will produce a 1½″ quilted circle. That means the actual opening measures 2″ across. Remember, you have to take into account the ¼″ distance from the needle to the edge of the ruler on both sides of the circle!

The Every Circle set quilts circles from ½″ to 7″. The Every Curve set takes over where the Every Circle set leaves off, giving you curves for circles measuring from 8″ to 12″. You can further augment your circle collection by using it in tandem with echo clips or guides (page 25).

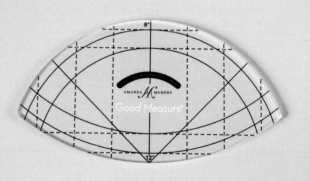

This ruler from my Good Measure Every Curve set quilts a portion of an 8″ circle on one side and a portion of a 12″ circle on the other.

With circle rulers on a domestic machine, it will become *really* apparent if you forget to hold the ruler with both hands because the pressure against the foot will cause the ruler to slip all over the place! Remember to hold a couple fingers from each hand on the ruler and a couple fingers on the fabric to prevent this from happening (see the photo, at right).

When using circles on both domestic machines and longarm, you will have to start and stop stitching more than you would with a straight ruler. *I might move my hands four times to get all the way around the external portion of a circle ruler!* Again, you'll know you aren't repositioning your hands enough if your ruler is slipping all over the place.

How to hold a circle ruler on a domestic machine. (For more about how to hold rulers on domestic machines, see Executing Rulerwork on a Domestic Machine, Step 7, page 107.)

Help! I Have Nested Circles!

If you have nested circles but from one piece of plastic, like those in the initial BERNINA sets, you can use painter's tape to bind them together and give you more surface area with which to work.

On the following pages are some of my favorite circle-based designs.

CONNECTING CORNERS

You aren't always going to quilt all the way around a circle. Many times, you will just want to use the ruler to connect corners.

For instance, with an antique hand-pieced quilt top, you might want to use a ruler to connect the corners of the blocks, because stitching over the seams might further weaken them. Or maybe you just want a quick and easy finish to a modern quilt.

Different sized circles will give you different looks.

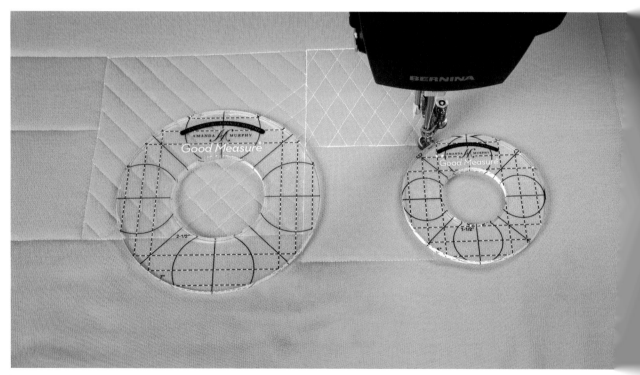

Quilt around the block if desired. Choose a ruler that will produce a curve that is a good size for your block. A smaller circle will quilt a deeper curve. A larger circle will quilt a shallower curve.

Starting in one of the block's corners, lower the foot and bring up the ruler so that it is snug against the foot. Remember, the edge of the ruler needs to be positioned ¼″ away from the corner toward which you are quilting ...

... because, if the edge of your ruler is right on top of the point you are trying to hit, the result will make you sad!

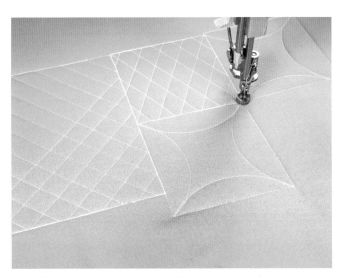

Quilt from corner to corner until you return to your starting point.

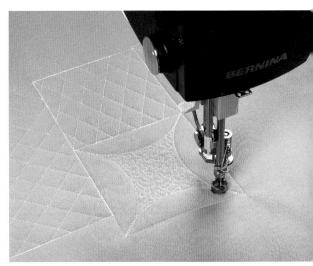

You can fill the area with free-motion to give the rulerwork more dimension!

What to Do If Your Circle Ruler Starts to Slip

Did I mention I'm not a fan of ripping? Well, I'm not. Sometimes you can cover up a mistake if you find it early enough, and no one will even notice!

If you notice your circle ruler has slipped just a little bit, don't despair!

Instead, stop, and reposition your ruler just a little bit. Quilt a few more stitches.

Correct your ruler placement a little more. Quilt a few more stitches.

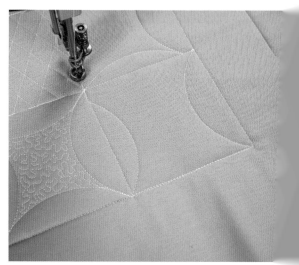

Continue quilting and correcting, until your ending point is dead-on. From a distance, it is more noticeable if you don't hit your corner than if the curve is a little irregular.

PEBBLES

A line of pebbles is a great way to give a quilt a more modern feel. (See *Sewing Room Sampler*, page 87, as an example!) It is much easier to quilt this motif using the interior portion of a circle ruler. That is why the internal circles on my Every Circle rulers go all the way up to 2½″.

Note: *If you have a longarm with a hopping foot that cannot be raised, I would recommend another style of circle ruler instead to execute this motif.*

Typically, I like to choose a circle motif that is slightly smaller than my sashing so I don't have to be quite so exact in my design placement. So, for a 2″ sashing, I would choose a circle ruler that quilts 1½″ circles.

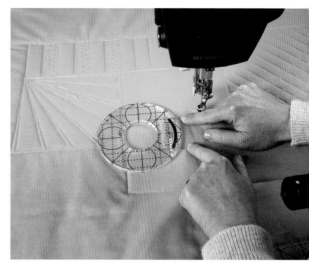

Note that the straight markings on the sides of the ruler will help you keep the circle motifs centered to the sashing.

If you don't have markings on the sides of your ruler, drawing a centerline on the fabric will help you stay centered to the sashing.

Begin at the edge of the sashing area. Quilt clockwise around the circle.

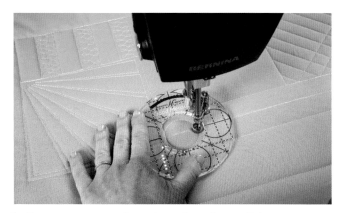

Return to your starting point and continue quilting on top of your previous stitches until you get to the opposite side of the circle. (You can note the centerline of the ruler for reference.)

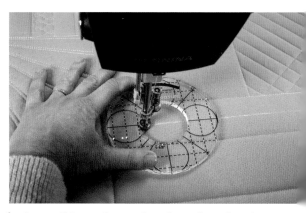

Stop quilting and move the ruler to the right to be in the position to quilt the next circle. Note that, on my Every Circle rulers, the previous quilting will be covered by the solid curved lines on the ruler. The Every Oval rulers work the same way.

Quilt around this circle in a counterclockwise direction.

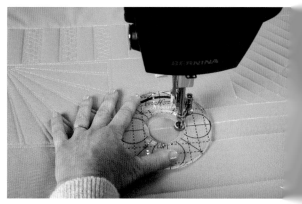

Return to your starting point and continue quilting on top of your previous stitches until you get to the opposite side of the circle.

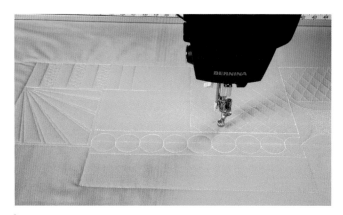

Continue, alternating the quilting direction of each circle until you have quilted an entire row of pebbles!

SCALLOPS

Scallops are a quick, classic design perfect for borders, and there are so many variations to explore!

You'll be quilting a half-circle, so pick a circle whose quilted radius is smaller than your border width. So, if the border is 2½″ wide, I might choose a ruler that stitches a 4″ external circle.

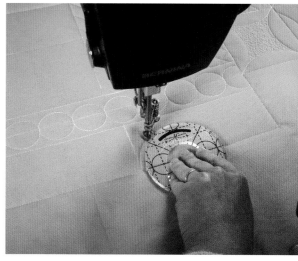

Quilt the border edges. Start in the center of the border and quilt half-circles along the border edge. The centerline of the ruler should lie right along the edge of the border.

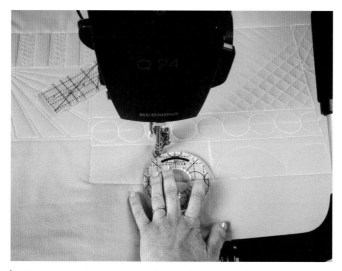

Continue quilting semicircles until you have filled the border. Then return to the border center and quilt the other side.

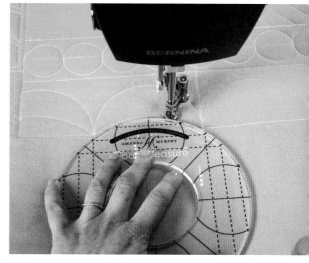

You can connect the bottom edges of the scallops using a larger circle ruler. (For really shallow curves, you might need to use the Every Curve ruler set.)

What if you have a narrow border and are looking to make a narrower design? Well, you could use a smaller ruler.

Or instead of quilting a full semicircle, you could use the lines on the edges of the ruler to quilt shallower curves.

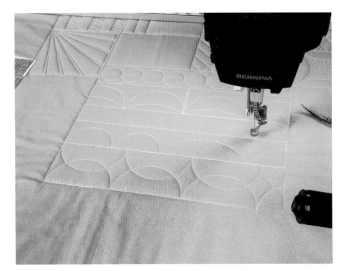

For wider borders, you can run scallops on both the top and bottom of border area, creating a design of interlocking petals and diamonds!

See my *Rulerwork Quilting Idea Book* for more design variations.

WAVES

I have another versatile design to show in my effort to convince you that circles are the most versatile design tool out there. Waves!

Draw a line through the horizontal center of your quilting area and make tic marks across it at standard intervals.

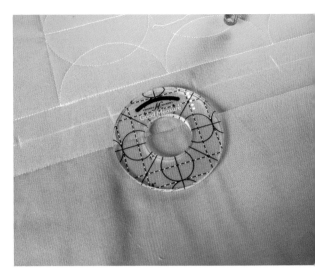

Audition circle rulers on top of the line to see what type of wave will result. A smaller circle will generate a deeper wave ...

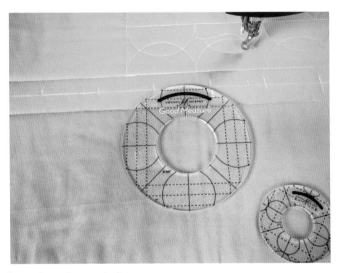

... than a larger circle.

Connect the marks, first holding the ruler under the line ...

↑ ... and then over the line.

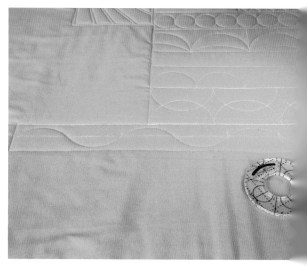

↑ Gradually, a wave emerges!

Want to make it eliminate some of the marking? If you line up the lines on the edges of an Every Circle ruler right on top of the line drawn through the center of the quilting area you don't even have to make tic marks! Simply quilt over the ruler ...

... and then under the ruler, making sure to align the same line on the ruler with the drawn line each time!

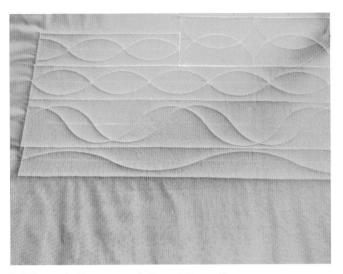

Want a shallower curve? Use a different line on the ruler or switch to a bigger circle size, like those contained in my Every Curve set!

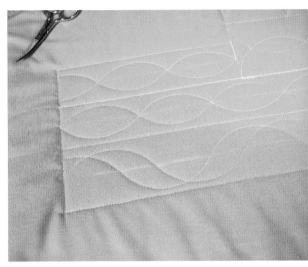

A second curve offset just a bit can produce a ribbon!

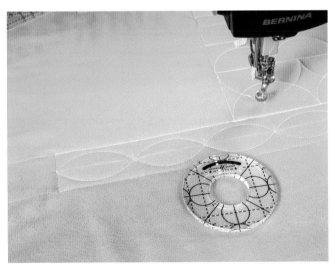

A second pass that is an exact mirror image produces a row of petals!

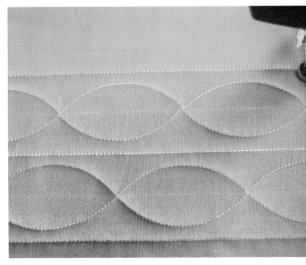

Why would you want to make the petal motif with two waves, rather than two rows of scallops? Because with two rows of scallops (the top row), it is hard to make the points meet!

BLOSSOMS

If you are looking to fill a large, empty block, you don't necessarily need a specialty ruler (although they are fun to play with). Your Circle or Oval sets can produce a large blossom motif in no time!

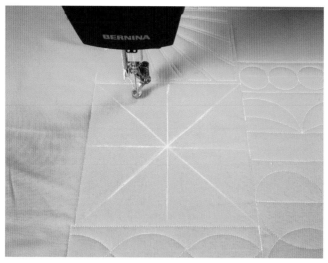

Draw horizontal and vertical lines through the quilting area, then add 45° lines.

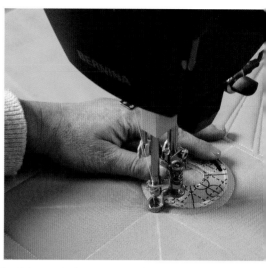

Select a circle appropriately sized to the shape you'd like to fill. Starting at the center mark and aligning the center of the circle ruler with the vertical line, stitch the first circle, coming back to the center mark.

Rotate the ruler and stitch another circle. Remember to stop and reposition your hands as needed.

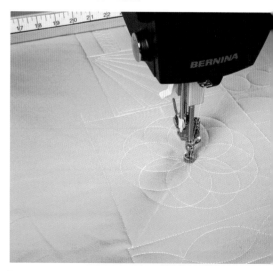

Continue the pattern to finish the medallion.

An easy way to echo this design is to use a bigger circle ruler or echo clips or guides (page 25).

In this variation, I used my Every Curve ruler set, but instead of quilting a full circle, I'm aligning one of the lines on the ruler with my alignment lines.

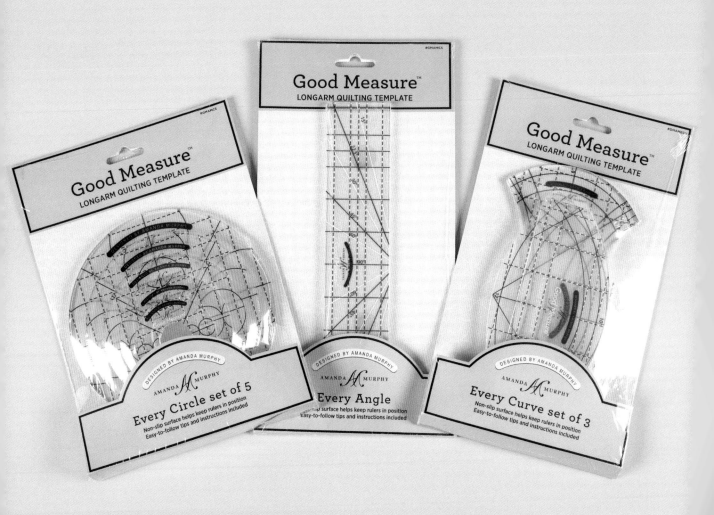

My favorite basic rulers: straight line, circles, and
curves—you can't go wrong with the basics!

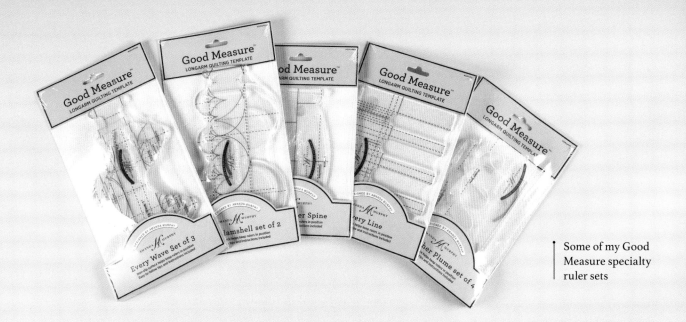

Some of my Good Measure specialty ruler sets

Specialty Rulers

Once you have mastered the basics, there is really no ruler shape that you can't handle!

Feel free to explore different brands and styles of rulers to find out what works best for you! I'm showing you examples from my line of rulers here, but there isn't any reason you can't apply these same techniques to any ruler out there.

Note that if you are using longer rulers on a smaller machine with a narrower throat space, you might have to rotate the quilt and work the design up and down, as opposed to left and right.

Rulerwork Stitch Length

When working with rulers, follow this general rule: As shapes gets smaller or curves get tighter, you should bring the stitch length down! You'll know your stitch length is too long on a small curvy motif if the quilted lines start to look like they have corners!

This stitch length might be okay for a larger motif, but it is too long for a 1″ clamshell.

Recommended Good Measure quilting ruler set: **EVERY WAVE**

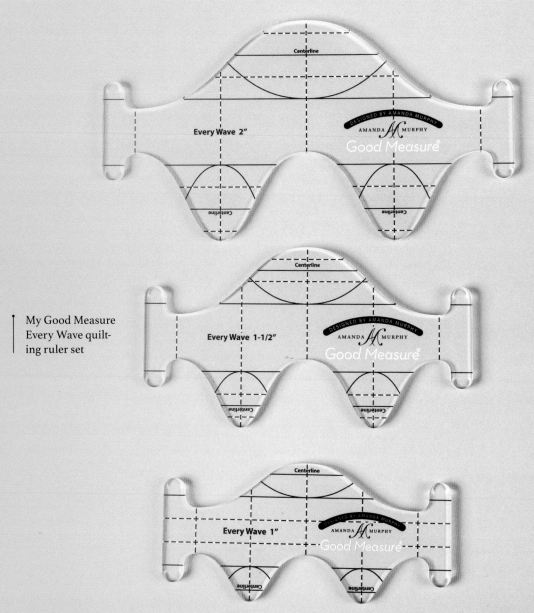

My Good Measure Every Wave quilting ruler set

A set of waves is a good choice if you make many quilts with sashing, as they are a quick and easy linear fill, but waves can also be used as an overall pattern.

My Every Wave set quilts waves that are 1″, 1½″, and 2″ in height, so they are the perfect size for sashing. The two sides of each ruler give you steeper and gentler waves of the same depth. If you need to fill a larger area, consider quilting two sets of waves that are either parallel or mirror images of each other!

Select a ruler whose curve depth is a little less than the height of the quilting area. Draw a line down the horizontal center of your quilting area with chalk or a wash-away fabric marker.

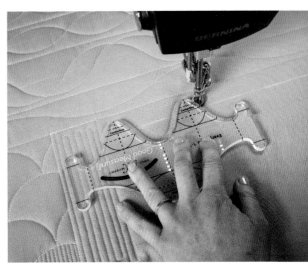

Starting at the center left edge of the quilting area, quilt from left to right, moving across the ruler. Make sure the centerline on the ruler is on top of the marked line on the fabric. (Note that the centerline doesn't look like it is in the center of the *ruler's curve*—because it isn't. But it *is* in the center of the resulting *quilted curve*, and that is what counts!)

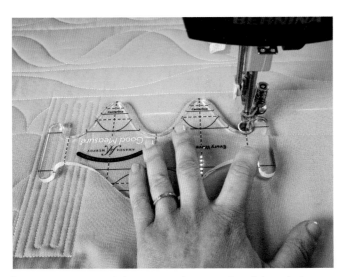

Don't quilt around the curve at the very edge of the ruler! It is just there to give you an exact stopping point.

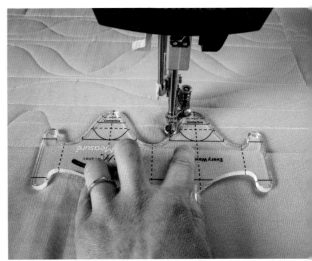

Reposition the ruler and continue quilting across the sashing, realigning the centerline of the ruler with the marked line on the fabric. (After you quilt across one of the sashing areas, you might find that there isn't a need to mark the other sashing areas, because you can use one of the other horizontal lines on the ruler for visual reference!)

If desired, quilt back from right to left offsetting the waves just a bit to produce a ribbon.

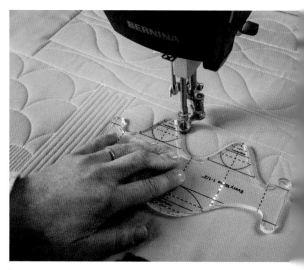

Or try lining up the curved lines on the ruler on top of the previously quilted lines for the second pass. I added these lines to the ruler because I'm not that great at positioning the second pass of this design. (Yes, I designed for my own challenges, but I hope this will make your quilting easier, too!)

You'll get a row of petals!

Recommended Good Measure quilting ruler set: **EVERY CLAMSHELL**

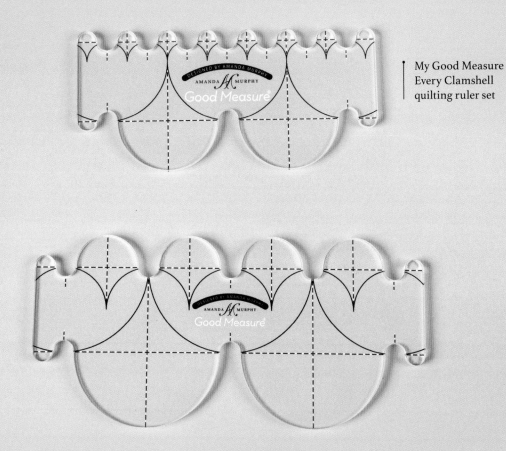

My Good Measure
Every Clamshell
quilting ruler set

Clamshells are a classic overall pattern that can quickly fill a quilt top. My Every Clamshell set gives you 1″, 2″, 3″, and 4″ clamshells. Of course, you can also quilt clamshells with a circle set, but a clamshell set allows you to quilt them quickly with no marking.

When quilted at a small scale, this pattern functions as a tight fill, like the type-A sister of free-motioned pebbles!

One caveat: On the BERNINA Q-Series, I prefer to use the #72 foot (rather than the #96 foot) to execute this design, because the profile of its sole is curved and therefore less likely to stick into the grooves of the ruler between the clamshells!

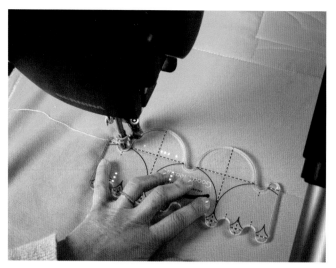

Starting at the bottom corner of the quilting area, bring up the ruler so that it is snug against the ruler foot. The horizontal line on the ruler should lie right on top of the edge of the quilting area.

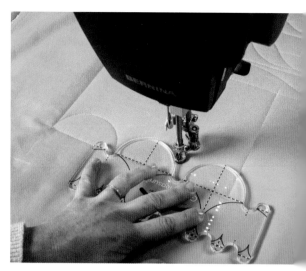

Quilt from left to right moving across the ruler, repositioning the ruler if needed.

When you are all the way across the row, travel up the side of the quilting area ...

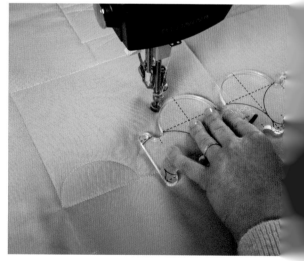

... and quilt back in the other direction. You'll know the ruler is in the right position when the solid lines on the ruler lay right on top of the previous stitches. (You might have to travel up or down the side of the quilting area just a bit to get into the right position.)

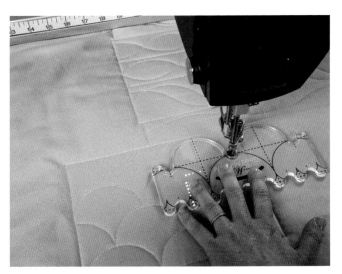

If you prefer, you can backtrack to the top of the clamshell you just quilted, rather than traveling along the edge of the quilting area, to start the next row.

Then backtrack to quilt the partial clamshell at the edge of the next row.

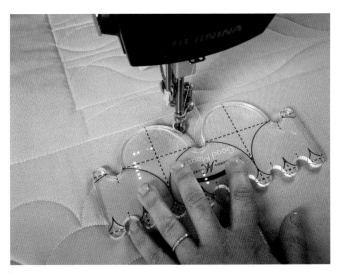

Continue quilting the next row of clamshells.

You'll frequently have some partial compensating motifs at the edge of the quilting area, and that is okay! Work your way back and forth until you have filled in the entire quilting area.

Recommended Good Measure quilting ruler set: **EVERY LINE**

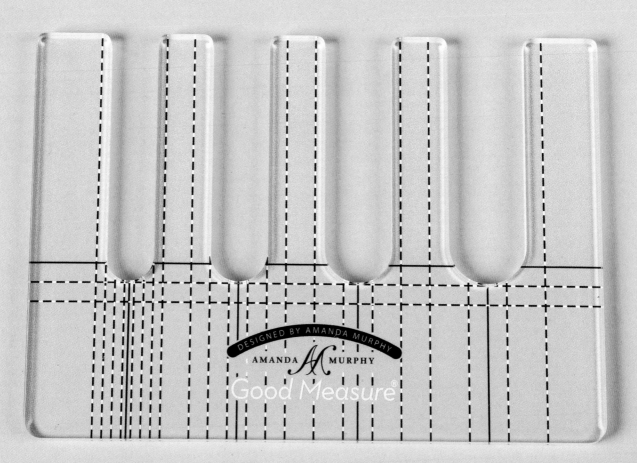

↑ My Good Measure Every Line quilting ruler

The Every Line ruler adds texture to quilting areas by giving you an easy way to produce a dense quilted fill.

The different slots in the ruler allow you to quilt lines ⅛″, ¼″, ⅜″, and ½″ apart.

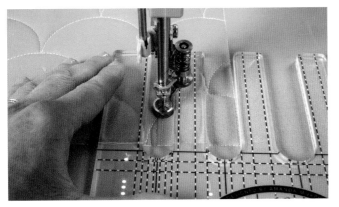

Bring your ruler up so that the right side of one of its slots is up against the right side of the foot. Quilt up the side of the ruler.

When you get to the top of the quilting area, shift the ruler over so that the left side of the slot is touching the left side of the foot.

Free-motion across to the other side of the ruler, so that the right side of the slot is touching the right side of the foot.

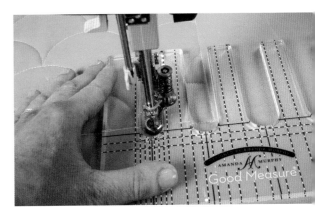

When you get to the bottom of the quilting area, shift over the ruler so that the left edge of the slot is again against the left edge of the ruler. Quilt back up the quilting area.

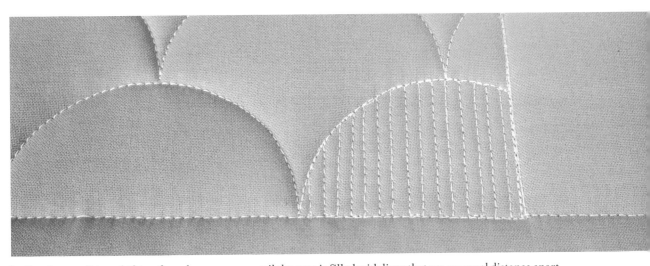

Continue quilting, shifting the ruler as you go, until the area is filled with lines that are an equal distance apart.

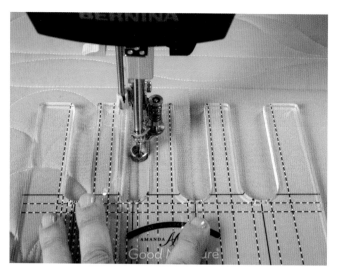

The lines at the bottom of the ruler help ensure that your quilting lines will be straight if you are filling a large quilted space. Simply make sure they lie right on top of the previous quilting as you work up and down the quilt.

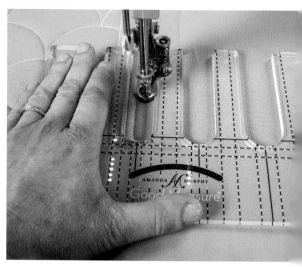

If you want curved lines at the top and bottom of this fill, you can use the curve at the bottom of the ruler to turn the corners. This takes a little more time, but produces a different look.

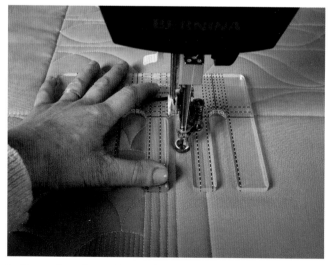

Rotate the ruler 180° to get the same curve at the top!

Recommended Good Measure quilting ruler sets: **EVERY FEATHER SPINE** • **EVERY FEATHER PLUME**

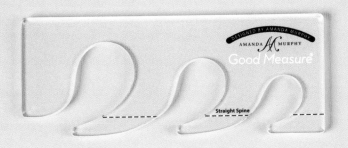

My Good Measure Every
Feather Spine and Every
Feather Plume quilting rulers

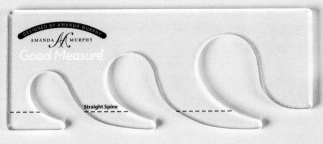

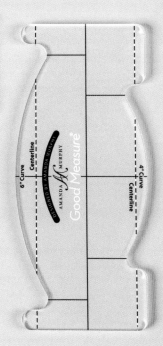

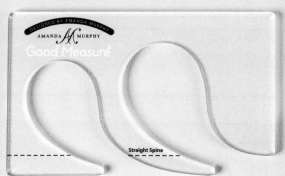

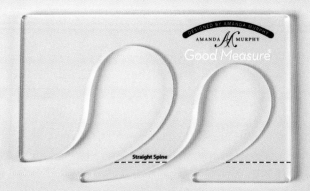

If you have ever struggled with learning to quilt feathers, a feather ruler set might be just what you need to get accustomed to quilting a plume shape! Regardless of the brand you choose, I really believe that the best method to quilt a feather with a ruler is the same method you would use to free-motion a feather—one with minimal backtracking.

There are many variations of feathers, but let me show you what I mean, using a feather border as an example....

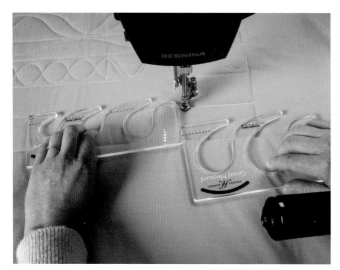

Quilt the edges of your border. Stitch a straight spine through the center of the border using the straight edge of one of the rulers. Starting on a side, line up the dashed line on the Every Feather Plume ruler over the spine. Select the ruler with the plume shape that is most appropriate to the border size.

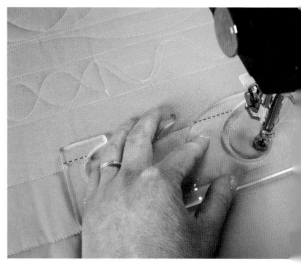

Note: You will quilt the plumes in pairs. Quilt over the top of a feathered plume about as far as shown. Be sure not to close the plume! You'll need to nest in the plume below it as you complete the border.

Bounce back to the top of the plume you just stitched as shown, quilting over your previous stitching line, until you reach a good branching-off point for the next plume.

Shift the ruler over so that it is positioned to make the next plume. Note that you are quilting only the *tops* of the plumes.

⬆ To finish the pair, quilt back down into the spine.

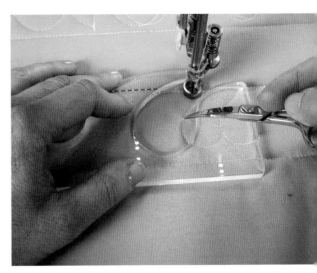

⬆ Travel a little further up the spine and place your ruler on it to check if you are in the correct position. Ideally when you line up the ruler, the previous plume will stick out just a little more than ¼″ from the ruler edge. Then you know that the new plume will touch the previous plume!

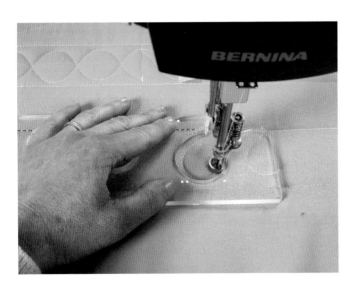

⬆ Quilt out from the spine to form the next plume, extending the arc until it touches the previous plume.

⬆ Quilt to the top of the plume over your previous stitching.

Branch off to make the next plume as shown, moving back into the spine.

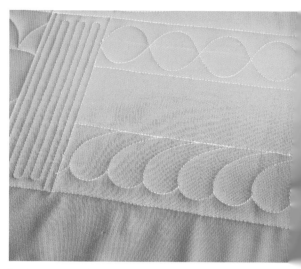

Continue quilting plumes in pairs until you have completed one side of the feather border. (Note that you might have to adjust the size of the plumes in the border corners. You can consult my *Organic Free-Motion Quilting Idea Book* for more examples of ways to quilt feathers.)

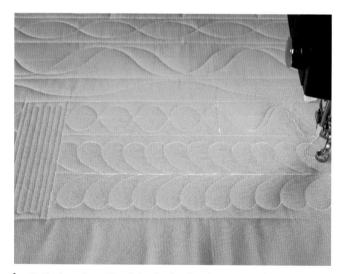

Quilt the other side of the feather border in a similar manner.

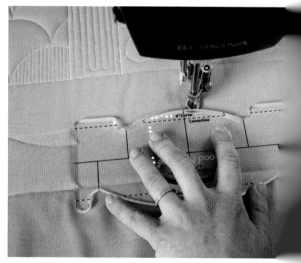

Laying the dashed line on the ruler right along the drawn line, quilt over the ruler ...

If you'd like to quilt a feathered border with a curvy spine, you can use my Every Spine Ruler to quilt the spine. Mark a horizontal line across the quilting area.

↑ ... and then under the ruler.

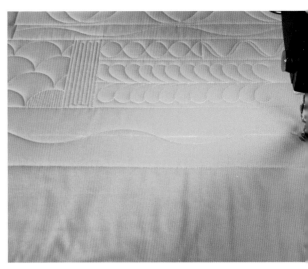

↑ Continue until you have finished your spine!

↑ Quilt plumes in a similar manner as the process shown (pages 66–68), but note that you'll have to fudge the alignment of the plume ruler a bit, disregarding the spine marking.

↑ With a curvy spine you might turn the ruler a bit when needed, and use a few different sizes of plumes when quilting!

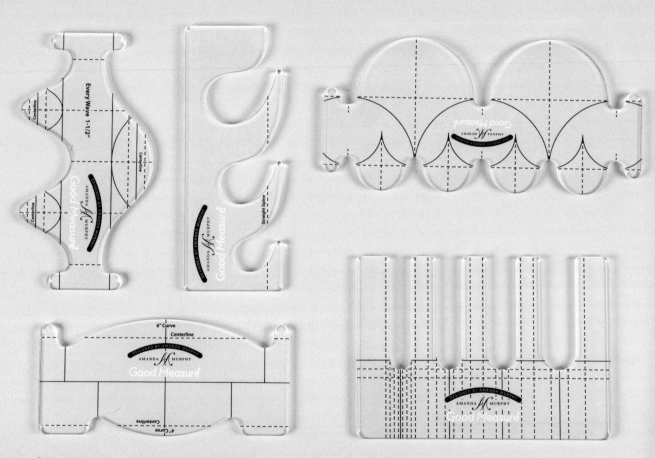

↑ Specialty rulers are a lot of fun to play with!

Planning a Quilt with Rulers

Many times the part of the quilting process that most intimidates people is figuring out what to quilt! They imagine professional quilters just have a fully formed quilting plan that pops into their heads like magic! Let me assure you this is not the case—at least, not for me or for the people I know. Most professional quilters spend time really planning out what they are going to quilt and the order in which they are going to do it. Of course, experience plays a role and, with time (and mistakes), you do become better at knowing what will work—but planning is always part of the process.

My free-motion students know that I'm not particular about every quilting line in my quilt top. I'm not a fan of ripping, so unless I could see a mistake "from a galloping horse," I'm probably leaving it in. And if I can't find my mistakes at the end of the day, I figure that they weren't worth ripping out in the first place. *But*, because my quilts hang at shows like Quilt Market and BERNINA University, I am a huge stickler for them hanging square and flat!

People all quilt differently. Although there is no one right way, I'm going to share with you my process that gets me clean and square results every time. Hopefully it will help you, too!

When I'm planning a quilt, I aim for a quilting density that is generally uniform across the entire quilt top. This doesn't mean that I won't have a loose feather next to a tiny stipple in some instances, but in general I won't plan one quadrant of the quilt to be filled with tiny pebbles while its neighbor is filled with really open quilting.

Of course, that is an exaggeration, but do you see what I'm getting at? That type of quilting plan will not result in a quilt that will hang square.

So I know that, for a custom quilt, if I build up the quilting density in just one area I must commit to that density for the majority of the quilt.

You can have a successful quilt that is loosely quilted and a successful quilt that is densely quilted, but it is next to impossible to get a quilt that is loosely quilted on one half and densely quilted on the other.

Detail of the densely quilted *BERNINA 125th Anniversary Quilt* (page 101). Frequently, custom quilts that combine rulerwork and free-motion are fairly densely quilted.

Photo by Amanda Murphy

Christmas Magic Sampler

This sampler is a loosely quilted quilt. Many pantograph-style (or repeating) designs are loosely quilted.

Photo by Amanda Murphy

On the same note, have you ever seen a rippled border? Experienced piecers know this can be caused by not measuring through the center of the quilt top when applying borders, but it can also definitely be caused by the quilting.

My *Winter Sports* quilt has a little bit of a wavy border—and I knew when I quilted it that it would end up with that wavy border. So why did I quilt it that way? Well, I was getting ready for a show and I had five days to get the entire piece made and quilted. But I had an idea that I really wanted to quilt "winter scenes" behind each athlete, and I knew that was going to take time. When it came time for the border, I had three hours to go before leaving for the airport. So I reluctantly put on a less densely quilted digital design through the border. I knew ahead of time it would ripple a bit, but I had to make a choice between it being a little rippled or not being finished at all. So I let it go—and I'm pretty sure that I was the only one who noticed (until I shared this little tidbit in this book!).

Winter Sports

This quilt has a little bit of a wavy border, but it is still one of my favorite quilts!

Photo by Amanda Murphy

Note: Keep It Consistent

The moral of the story is that if you commit to dense quilting in some areas of the quilt top, you should commit to dense quilting in all areas of the quilt top!

To explore quilting plans, I start with a fine marker and a diagram or photograph of the quilt. Make sure that any images you copy are clearly marked as legal to use for that purpose, so that you aren't stealing any designs! (*Note: The diagrams in this book are copyright protected.*)

If I am using a photograph, I try to get it pretty square but don't worry if it is a little off—this is going to be more of a mental note for me, so it doesn't have to be perfect. You can also place a sheet of plastic over the diagram/photo and draw on it.

Then I figure out my design. Assuming it is custom quilted, this might involve quilting-in-the-ditch and other rulerwork. So, this would be the time to pull out your rulers and see what you have that might work. It might also be a good opportunity to think about what rulers you might want to add to your "ruler stash." Generally, I recommend ones that you think you could use on multiple quilt tops.

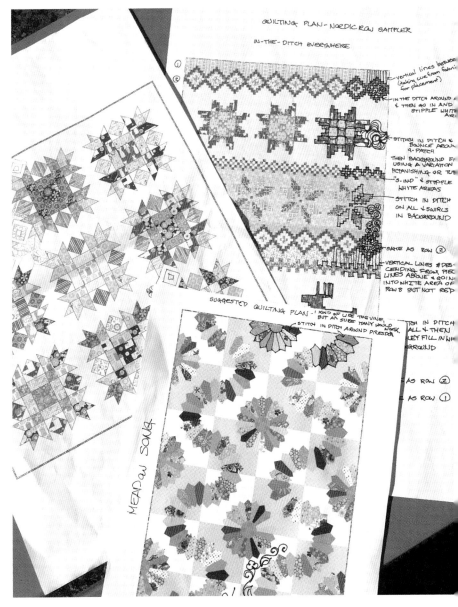

Some samples of my hand-drawn quilting plans

Photo by Amanda Murphy

TIP Drawing on the quilt layout in a scaled-down format forces me to consider it as a whole, which results in a more coherent design plan.

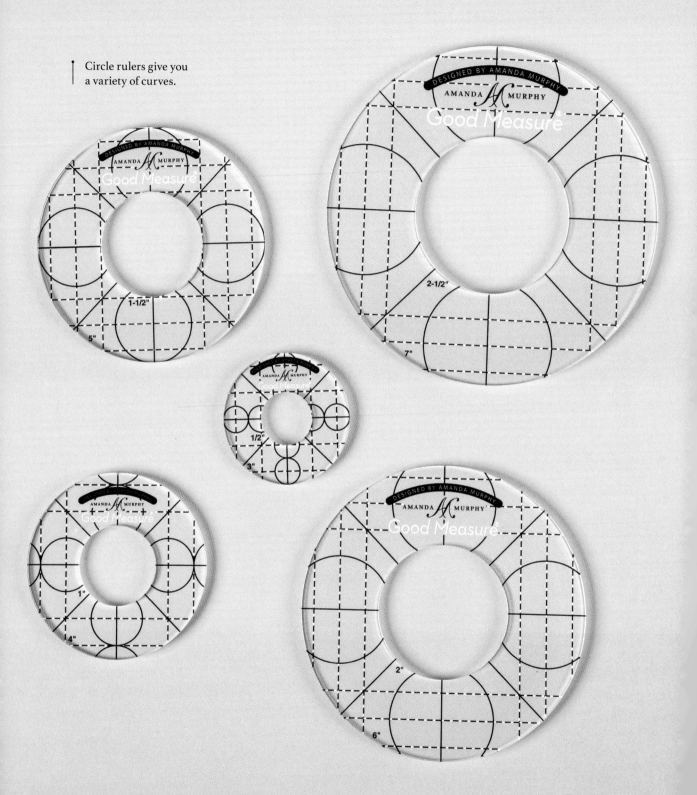

Circle rulers give you
a variety of curves.

TIP In general, if I quilt a certain motif in one area of my quilt, I like to have it appear in at least two other areas. That visual repetition helps guide your eyes across the quilt top and creates a cohesive look.

If I have a quilt with 6″ blocks and I want to connect the corners of those blocks, I'd look through my stash for a curved or circle ruler that spans 6″.

If I am connecting the corners of 2″ blocks, however, then it is helpful to have smaller circle rulers. (I'll say it again … you can *never* go wrong with a good set of circles!) Too big a circle would look like a straight line on a small block. Remember, the smaller the circle, the deeper the curve (page 42).

❜ Connecting corners, using a circle ruler

Note: Want More Rulerwork?
For more rulerwork designs, consult my Rulerwork Quilting Idea Book.

Note: Want More Free-Motion?
For more free-motion ideas, consult my Free-Motion Quilting Idea Book *and my* Organic Free-Motion Quilting Idea Book.

I also use my diagram to figure out any free-motion fills that I might want to incorporate. Generally, I don't draw all my free-motion quilting everywhere because that would take too much time. Instead, I try out a few things in different areas of the diagram and then go with the one I like best.

If you have a tablet, you can also use a variety of graphics programs to draw on a digital image of your quilt top.

Remember, the point of the diagram is for you to develop your ideas. No one will ever see these unless you write a book on the subject!

Once I've settled upon the design, I go back through and number each step. Be sure not to skip this part of the process—it is really important! It helps me ensure that my end result is a square quilt. Plus, if I put the quilt away for any amount of time, it helps me remember where I am in the process.

IN GENERAL, HERE ARE MY STEPS FOR QUILTING A CUSTOM QUILT ...

1. Baste the edges of the quilt top in the area to be covered by binding. When quilting on a domestic machine, baste around the entire top. When quilting on a longarm, you'll baste each area as you come to it.

2. Quilt the "bones" of the quilt. This includes any stitch-in-the-ditch (or "along-the-ditch") lines. It also includes any big rulerwork motifs that might help establish the divisions of negative space, like triangles or diamonds in a border. For an appliqué quilt, this might involve quilting around large appliqué shapes.

3. Quilt the medium fills. This includes any medium-scale free-motion fills and any similarly scaled rulerwork motifs.

4. Quilt the small fills. This might include motifs like pebbles or really small clamshells. Saving this step until last helps keep the surrounding areas nice and flat, since there is already quilting from Steps 1 and 2 securing those areas.

These steps might vary a bit depending upon whether I'm quilting on a longarm or a domestic, but in principle they are the same.

For more about the steps for quilting ...

... on a longarm, see Executing Rulerwork on a Longarm Machine (page 117).

... on a domestic, see Executing Rulerwork on a Domestic Machine (page 102).

Ready to see some examples?

Often my "in-the-ditch" quilted lines are actually "along-the-ditch" quilted lines—meaning I stitch a hairline toward one fabric, right along the seam. This places less stress on the seam, and the quilted lines tend to melt right into the sandwich!

Photo by Amanda Murphy

Creating a Coherent Design

If possible, I like to create quilting plans where the quilting accentuates the piecing. With rulers, you don't have to be an expert quilter to achieve this!

Diamond Jubilee

I used my Every Angle straight-line ruler to quilt rays that draw your eyes to the center of the quilt top. I also used my Every Circle set to help quilt around the center circle. Note how the free-motion in the background of the quilt contrasts and augments the impact of the straight-line quilting.

Photo by Amanda Murphy

Amethyst Jubilee

This quilt also utilizes lines made with a straight ruler to emphasize the piecing in a similar manner.

Sunrise

I used straight-line quilting in combination with simple loops to enhance the directional nature of the design. The quilting draws your eyes up and out from the Dresden Plates.

Celestial Lights Ruler Panel

This quilt uses the Every Oval ruler set in a myriad of ways, but the repetition of shapes also serves to guide your eye across the piece.

Fa La La Latte place mats

In these place mats, I used Every Angle, Every Circle, and Every Curve ruler sets to emphasize the blocks, and I added texture with free-motion. Note that I chose to quilt crosshatching on a diamond print so that I'd have to do less marking!

Photo by Amanda Murphy

Meadow Minis

I developed this quilt-as-you-go style design specifically to teach rulerwork. Simple curved and straight rulers are used throughout, resulting in a unified design.

Photo by C&T Publishing

Quilting the "Bones" of the Quilt

So what should you quilt first? People have been told all sorts of hard-and-fast rules—such as, "You should always quilt from the center out on a domestic machine." In my experience, that won't always give you the squarest result. You have to treat each quilt differently, using your common sense. Think ... *Are there any lines that, if they were not straight, would really stand out from a distance?* A lot of times, they are the borders or the sides of the blocks or even the sashing on a medallion quilt.

Let's consider a column of Flying Geese. You should first stitch-in-the-ditch all the way down the seam that joins the sashing to the blocks before stitching around or within the Geese.

The order of quilting is important!

Quilting the "bones" of a quilt can mean different things depending on the quilt's design. Here are some examples. ...

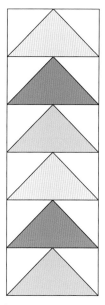

If you quilt around the entire block before going in to stitch the sides of the triangles, you will have a square result ...

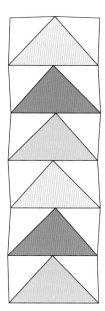

... but if you stitch the Geese first, the pull on the fabric from the seams will give the edges of those blocks a "wonky" look.

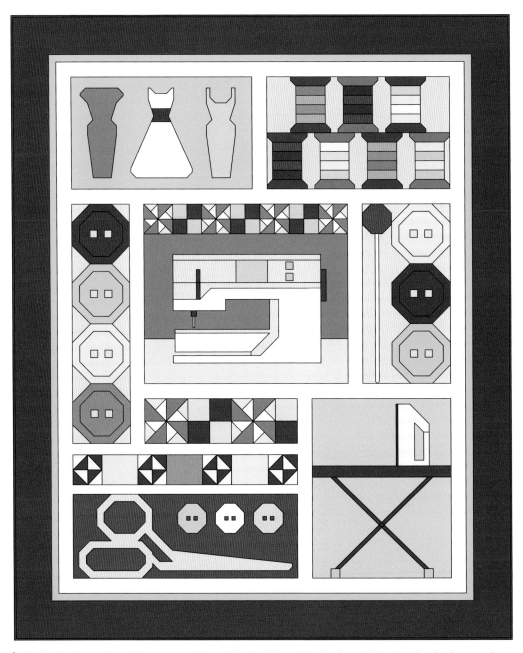

In *Sewing Room Sampler* (next page), I consider the "bones" to be the stitching-in-the-ditch around and inside the blocks and around the border. On a domestic, I'd go around the border first. I'd then make sure to go around each block completely before traveling into its interior to prevent seams from pulling and resulting in blocks that don't look square. On a longarm, I'd quilt around the border and the blocks as far as I could, then roll the quilt and repeat, until I got to the bottom of the quilt. Then I'd work back up the quilt with the medium fills, and so on.

Sewing Room Sampler

Photo by Amanda Murphy

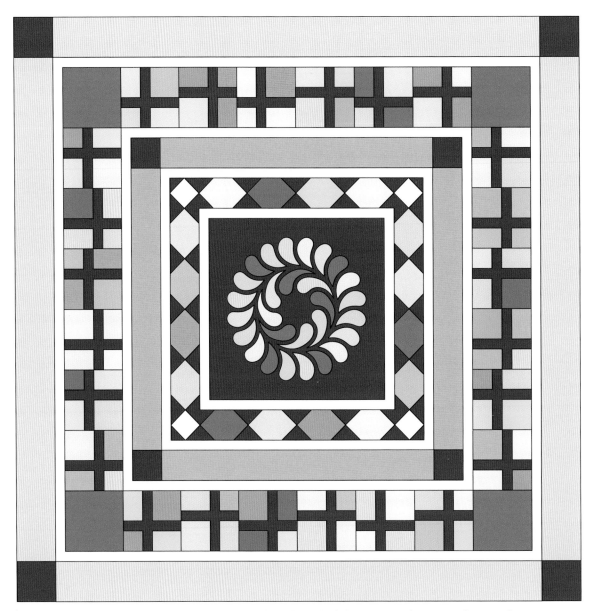

Plume (next page), is a typical medallion-style quilt, and I quilted the square sashing areas first. Working on a domestic machine, I started from the center sashing square and moved outward, quilting each sashing square in turn. Then I went in and quilted the divisions between the blocks. Think of how much messier it would have looked if I had quilted the blocks before securing the sashing areas!

Plume

Photo by Amanda Murphy

I wanted to include *Platinum Jubilee* (next page) in this book because it was an example of a quilt that would have been a disaster if I hadn't quilted the borders before the checkerboard sashing! If I had quilted the sashing first, the push and pull of the seams would have resulted in a border that looked far from straight! On a domestic, I would quilt all the way around the border first. On a longarm, I would quilt the border as I came to it, and then move into the interior of the quilt top.

Platinum Jubilee

Photo by Amanda Murphy.

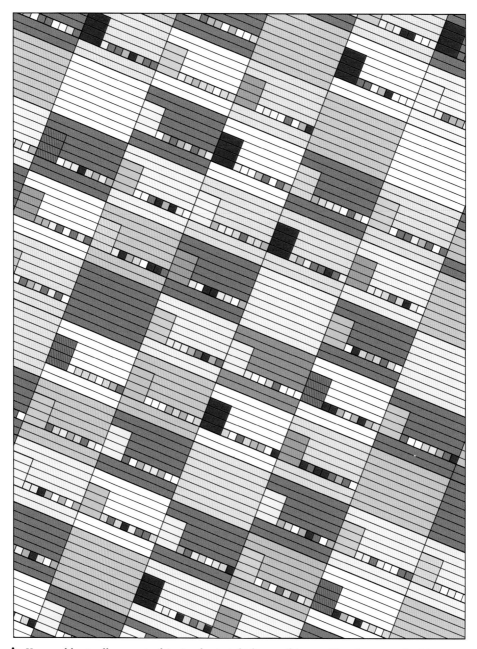

You could actually execute this simple straight-line quilting on *Slope* (next page) with a straight ruler, like my Every Angle, or with a walking foot, but I wanted to include it here to show how important it is to keep the quilting density consistent throughout the process. To keep this quilt square, I quilted the long lines along the quilt's seams first, and then kept subdividing the areas between them until I got quilted lines that were about ½″ apart. As I subdivided the lines, I also reversed the direction of my quilting. If, instead, I had started in the center and quilted a line ½″ away on the bottom and ½″ away on the top, and just kept adding lines from the center out, pretty soon the quilt would have started to bow out at the ends. I would have never gotten a square result. Remember, the "center out" rule isn't hard and fast!

Slope

Photo by Amanda Murphy

In *Diamond Jubilee* (page 79), I'd consider the "bones" of this quilt to be the cream sashing that makes up the medallion. On a domestic, you could definitely start with the center circle and quilt outward, securing the cream sashing as you worked out. On a longarm, however, you'd have to quilt a bit of the free-motion background just to get down to the medallion. Otherwise, the unsecured background would fold up on the bars of the machine. At the end, you could fill in the rest of the background with more free-motion quilting.

Combining Ruler Shapes

I frequently use more than one ruler for my quilts. In fact, sometimes I use a bunch!

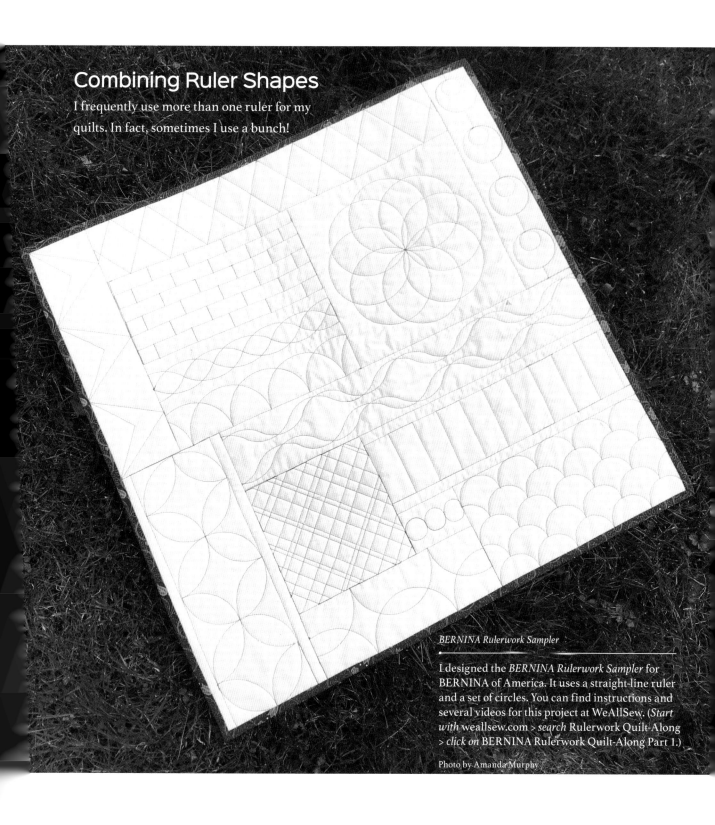

BERNINA Rulerwork Sampler

I designed the *BERNINA Rulerwork Sampler* for BERNINA of America. It uses a straight-line ruler and a set of circles. You can find instructions and several videos for this project at WeAllSew. (*Start with* weallsew.com > *search* Rulerwork Quilt-Along > *click on* BERNINA Rulerwork Quilt-Along Part 1.)

Photo by Amanda Murphy

Good Measure Rulerwork Sampler

I used my first eight sets of Good Measure rulers to quilt my *Good Measure Rulerwork Sampler*. You can see how I divided the space in a downloadable PDF (Good Measure Rulerwork Sampler) on my website (see About the Author, page 127). You can find videos of these rulers in use on my YouTube channel. If you don't have all my rulers, you can still quilt the sampler—just fill in any empty spaces with your own designs!

Combining Rulerwork with Free-Motion

As you begin to quilt more of your own projects, you'll gain confidence. One day, you'll think, "If I could fill the background with stipples or loops, that will make my rulerwork stand out a little more." And guess what? You'll be free-motion quilting before you know it! It doesn't even need to be fancy motifs to be impressive. Free-motion quilting and rulerwork go hand-in-hand, and together they *sing*!

Sewing Room Sampler (full quilt, page 87) is a great example of rulerwork and free-motion being combined in a way that is both modern and fun! I used different free-motion fills in each block, but it is the rulerwork in elements like the crosshatching and the pebbled sashing that unifies the design!

Photo by Amanda Murphy

Combining Rulerwork with Digitized Designs

If you have a longarm with automation, or if you own a domestic machine capable of embroidery, you can push the envelope even further. In the following quilts, I've combined rulerwork, free-motion, and digitized designs. For me, the integration of many techniques is what defines quilting at the beginning of the twenty-first century!

I've digitized many collections of quilting motifs for OESD for both longarm and embroidery machines. They can be purchased through your local quilt shop—or go to my website (page 127) and click on Amanda's Quilting Collections Digitized for Domestic Embroidery Machines and Longarms.

A sampling of blocks from my Quilting Collections from OESD, digitized for longarms and domestic embroidery machines.

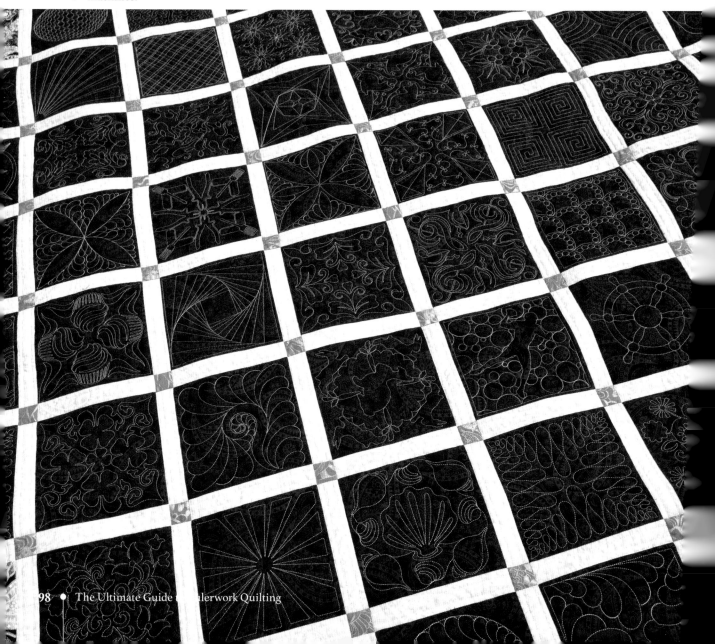

Meadow Blooms

Rulerwork defines the shapes and fools the eye into thinking the blocks are floating on top of the background. Rulerwork also adds interest to the border area. The free-motion motifs give the quilt texture—but it hardly matters what the motifs are, as it is difficult to see them on the gray background. Digitized motifs give uniformity to the blocks.

Photo by Amanda Murphy

Detail of *Platinum Jubilee* (page 91). I used rulers for all the stitch-in-the-ditch or "along-the-ditch" work, free-motion ribbon candy for the sashing, and a digitized motif from my quilting collections for OESD.

Photo by Amanda Murphy

BERNINA 125th Anniversary Quilt

In 2018, I was honored to design the *BERNINA 125th Anniversary Quilt*, along with a coordinating fabric line. I used my BERNINA Jubilee Ruler Set to travel around the embroideries and quilt details in the main blocks. Digitized quilting motifs from my Jubilee Embroidery Collection are used in the border. They are surrounded by free-motion quilting. You can find instructions for this quilt at WeAllSew. (*Start with* weallsew.com > *search* Anniversary Quilt-Along Part 1 > *click on* BERNINA 125th Anniversary Quilt-Along: Part 1 [September 10, 2018].)

Photo by Amanda Murphy

Executing Rulerwork on a Domestic Machine

TIP A practice sandwich is invaluable! Always quilt a little test piece before you start on your actual project! This will allow you to test your thread tension and other settings before you start on your final piece.

A Domestic Rulerwork Primer

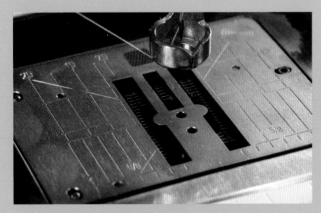

Lower the feed dogs on the machine. On BERNINAs, the feed dogs actually turn off when you lower them. If you have a machine where the feed dogs do not turn off, lower the stitch length as far down as it can go to minimize vibration.

Spread a Free Motion Glider or Supreme Slider (page 21) on the bed of the machine, if desired.

Your Movements and Machine Settings Determine the Stitch Length

The good news is that once you master stitch regulation for rulerwork, you'll be a lot better at controlling it when you're free-motion quilting. I actually do a lot of my free-motion quilting with my BERNINA Adjustable Ruler Foot #72 so that I can easily switch to rulerwork and then back again!

Three factors determine your stitch length on a domestic machine:

• The speed at which you move your hands.

• The speed slider on the machine.

• How much pressure you use on the foot pedal.

If you achieve stitches that are pretty good 80% of the time, that is **excellent***! Give yourself a pat on the back. You are not a computer, and your quilting will have special value because it was done by a person!*

If you are comfortable with the speed at which you are moving your hands, but your stitches are too long, you need more stitches per inch. You can accomplish this by moving up the speed slider on the machine or pushing on the foot pedal a bit harder.

If you are comfortable with the speed at which you are moving your hands, but your stitches are too short, you need fewer stitches per inch. You can accomplish this by moving down the speed slider on the machine or pushing on the foot pedal a bit less.

Many people who struggle to find a consistent quilting speed find it helpful to set their speed slider lower and floor the foot pedal.

Bring the quilt sandwich over to the machine. Lower the presser foot. Adjust the height of the ruler foot so that its sole just skims the surface of the quilt sandwich.

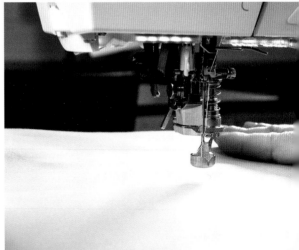

If there is significant distance between the quilt sandwich and the foot, it will result in skipped stitches.

If the foot is so low that it makes an impression on the quilt sandwich, it will be very difficult to move the fabric.

Starting and Stopping Threads: The Modern Method

STEP 1

Bring the bobbin thread up through the quilt. Do this by holding onto the top thread and bringing the presser foot down.

↑ Lower the needle.

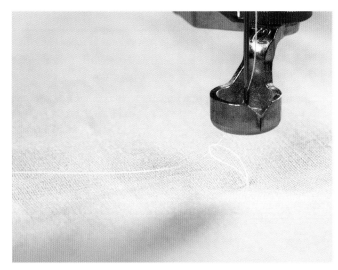

Bring the needle up, and bring up the presser foot. Pull on the top thread to bring the bobbin thread up.

↑ Hold onto both threads.

STEP 2

↑ Lower the presser foot and needle.

STEP 3

↑ Bring the ruler over snug against the foot. *Important: Be sure* **never** *to bring up the ruler before the presser foot is down!*

STEP 4

↑ Edge the quilting line into position so it is ¼″ away from the edge of the ruler. You can cut a little ¼″ piece of quilting plastic or paper to help with this until you get used to eyeballing a ¼″ measurement. (Believe me, once you do a few quilts with rulers, that part will be easy!)

STEP 5

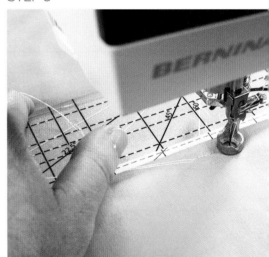

↑ Holding both the top and bobbin threads, take a few stitches *very* close together to lock the threads.

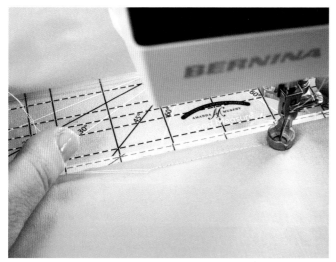

Gradually increase the stitch length so that it *looks* like it is between a 2.5 and 3.0 for a loose or medium design like a straight line or gentle curve, or between a 2.0 and 2.5 for a steeper curve.

Clip the starting threads right at the quilt sandwich.

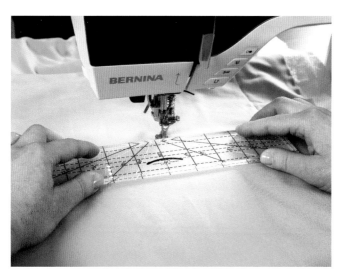

You can hold the ruler in front of the foot ...

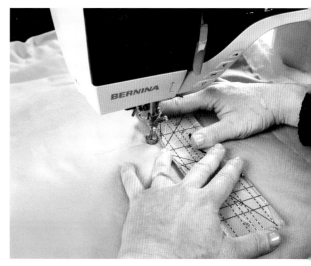

... you can hold the ruler to the side of the foot ...

... or you can hold the ruler behind the foot. But no matter which way you hold it or which direction you sew, make sure that a couple fingers from each hand are on the ruler and a couple of fingers from each hand are on the fabric for maximum stability!

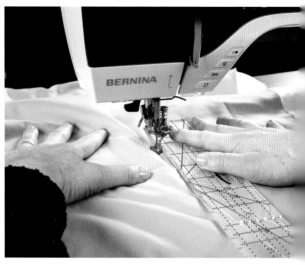

If, instead, you hold one hand on the ruler and the other on the fabric, there will be a lot of torque. And even if you can get away with it when quilting with a straight ruler ...

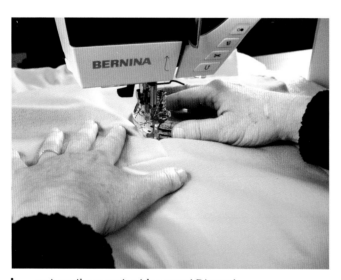

... wait until you try it with a curve! *Disaster!*

Holding the ruler on the curved edge of a sewing table is also not a good idea!

STEP 8

Remember, whether you are using a straight or curved ruler, the ruler's edges should be ¼″ away from the point you are trying to hit!

STEP 9

Continue quilting at a normal stitch length until you are ready to end your threads. To do so, quilt a few stitches close together and, bringing up the needle and presser foot, grab onto the thread coming out of the needle.

STEP 10

Hold onto this top thread and take one more stitch.

Pull on both the loop of thread that you are holding and the thread coming out of the needle to bring the bobbin thread up through the quilt sandwich.

Move the quilt at least 1″ away from its original position and clip the threads at the surface. This will leave the bobbin thread longer and make it easier to bring to the top of the quilt the next time.

When Stopping and Restarting, Don't "Jump" Your Machine!

When you stop, reposition your hands, and start to move again, it is very easy to start moving your hands at the exact same time you press the foot pedal—and that will result in a long jump stitch!

Instead, it should feel like you push the foot pedal first, and *then* move your hands. Make sure you see the needle move before you start moving your hands. In fact, I'd rather see you take a stitch in place before moving your hands rather than having a big jump stitch. This delay will seem awkward at first, but soon it will become second nature.

Incidentally, this same technique will also help you prevent jump stitches when free-motion quilting.

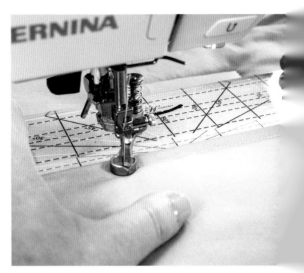

A big, bad jump stitch.

Starting and Stopping Threads for Show Quilts

For show quilts, whether you are on a longarm or domestic machine, you should not use the modern method of ending and starting threads.

STEP 1

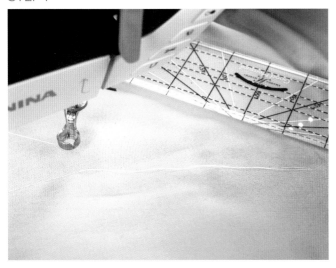

Instead, leave both the top and bottom thread about 4″ long when you both begin and end any stitching.

STEP 2

Later, go back and knot these threads near the surface of the quilt sandwich as you would a French knot.

STEP 3

Thread a chenille or self-threading needle with the thread ends and run the needle through the quilt sandwich so that the needle pops out 1″ or so away. Pull on the threads until the knot pops into the quilt sandwich.

STEP 4

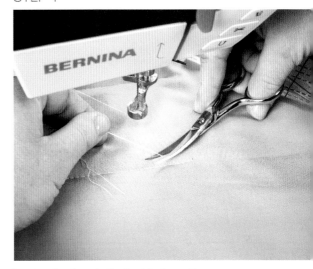

Clip the threads flush with the quilt top.

Amanda's Steps for Custom Quilting on a Domestic Machine

Keeping the quilting density uniform throughout ensures a neat and square result.

1. Take a picture of the quilt and make a few copies. Draw with a marker on the copies until you develop a quilting plan that you like. (If you are using one of my panels, the guide has the quilting plan.)

2. Spray or pin baste the quilt sandwich.

3. Machine baste all the way around the sandwich through all layers, about ⅛˝ from the edge of the quilt top.

4. Do all the quilting-in-the-ditch using the straight ruler, removing the pins as necessary. Make sure to quilt in different directions so you don't end up with a diamond-shaped quilt! (To figure out what to quilt first, see Quilting the "Bones" of the Quilt, page 85.)

5. Do all other rulerwork.

6. Quilt large-scale free-motion motifs.

7. Quilt medium-scale free-motion motifs.

8. Quilt small-scale free-motion motifs.

Baste Well

Regardless of your basting method, baste well to get your quilt square! Don't undo your hard work of squaring up the quilt by starting to quilt in the middle and then "smoothing out" the backing fabric as you quilt outward. This will push the backing outward, and the quilt will lose its squared-up shape!

Ergonomic Tips for Domestic Machines

When quilting on a domestic machine, the movement should stem from your upper arms—not your wrists! This will both be kinder to your body *and* make your shapes smoother. It is much harder to make jerky movements if you are not quilting in your wrists.

Additionally, if you have adjusted your chair so that it is a good height for the sewing table or cabinet, make sure that your feet aren't dangling above the ground. It is hard to have good posture if your knees are much lower than your hips. I usually put my foot pedal on a yoga block so that it is at a comfortable height for me.

Make sure you have glasses that allow you to see the sewing area without hunching; be aware that your sewing focal length might be different from your reading focal length.

Take breaks! Set your phone alarm to take a break for a few minutes every hour. Get a glass of water. Stretch your shoulders by pulling on the bottom of the chair while straightening your back. Or lean forward while pulling your shoulders back, bracing your arms on the sides of a doorway.

Photo by BERNINA International

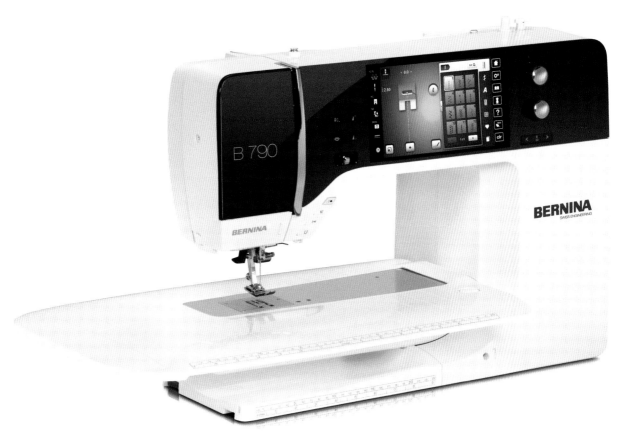

Domestic Rulerwork Troubleshooting

DOMESTIC PROBLEM 1: MY THREAD TENSION IS OFF.

Possible solutions:

- Your upper thread is not seated properly in the tension discs. Rethread.

- Your bobbin tension is too tight or too loose for the thread you are using. Adjust accordingly.

- Your top tension is too tight or too loose for the thread you are using. Adjust accordingly.

- Your bobbin is seated or wound incorrectly. Try another bobbin.

- You are using a specialty thread that requires a different thread in the bobbin. Consult the manufacturer for their bobbin thread recommendations.

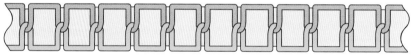

Correct thread tension

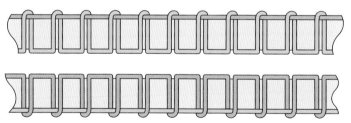

Incorrect thread tension

DOMESTIC PROBLEM 2: MOST OF MY THREAD TENSION IS GOOD, *BUT* I HAVE PROBLEMS AT THE CORNERS OF MY DESIGNS.

- *Solution:* Quilt two stitches on top of each other when changing directions. This will lock the threads and make pulled stitches less likely to occur.

DOMESTIC PROBLEM 3: MY THREAD KEEPS BREAKING *OR* I'M GETTING SKIPPED STITCHES.

Possible solutions:

- Your ruler foot is too high.

- Your machine has too much lint buildup. Treat it to a thorough cleaning.

- Your machine needs oil. (Not all machines take oil—consult your dealer if you have questions.)

- Your needle is not the appropriate size for the thread you are using. Change your needle to a larger size or try a topstitch needle, which has a larger eye.

- There is a burr on your needle or it has gotten dull. Change your needle.

- Try a thread stand.

- If you are using a specialty thread, a bit of silicone can sometimes help tame it.

- You might have a bad (or just old!) spool of thread. Switch to another spool and see if the problem continues.

DOMESTIC PROBLEM 4: I AM HAVING DIFFICULTY MOVING THE FABRIC.

- *Solution:* Your foot is mounted too close to your fabric and is impeding its movement. Adjust the foot's height (see For Domestics *and* Longarms, page 19).

DOMESTIC PROBLEM 5: MY RULER IS SLIPPING!

Possible solutions:

- Make sure you have some fingers of both hands on the ruler and some fingers of both hands on the fabric (see pages 107 and 108).

- Make sure you are applying pressure only to the flat portion of the sewing surface. (Don't hold the ruler off the flat surface or it might tip; see page 108.)

- Be sure not to try to quilt too far a distance before you stop and reposition your hands. Stop and reposition your hands before you lose control!

- If you are using nested rulers, tape a few together for more surface area (see Help! I Have Nested Circles!, page 41).

DOMESTIC PROBLEM 6: MY STITCHES ARE TOO LONG.

- *Solution:* You need more stitches per inch. Move up the speed slider on your machine or push the foot pedal a bit harder.

DOMESTIC PROBLEM 7: MY STITCHES ARE TOO SHORT.

- *Solution:* You need fewer stitches per inch. Move down the speed slider on your machine or push the foot pedal a bit less.

DOMESTIC PROBLEM 8: MY QUILT TOP IS SHAPED LIKE A DIAMOND.

- *Solution:* You have probably quilted mostly in one direction. Try quilting in a different directions next time.

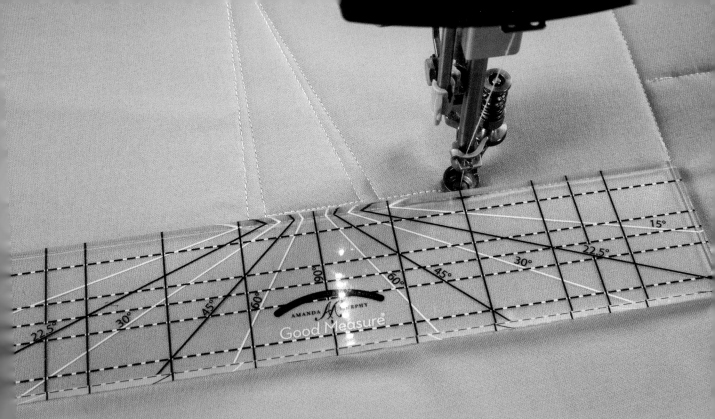

Executing Rulerwork on a Longarm Machine

Rulerwork can be easier on longarms because:

• You don't have to move the fabric in tandem with the ruler. Instead, you are moving the machine.

• You often have stitch regulation! (Of course, if you have a BERNINA Q 20 Sit-Down Longarm Quilting Machine, you'll have stitch regulation on that as well!)

 TIP A practice area is really beneficial! If you have a little extra backing fabric, make it extra wide so that you can have areas in which to warm up and test settings as you work down the quilt!

A Longarm Rulerwork Primer

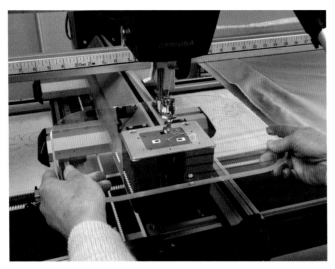

↑ Put on the ruler table and ruler foot.

↑ Bring the bobbin thread up through the quilt. Do this by holding onto the top thread and bringing your presser foot down, needle down, needle up, and presser foot up again. Pull on the top thread to bring up the bobbin thread. Hold onto both threads.

STEP 2

↑ Lower the presser foot and needle.

STEP 3

↑ Bring the ruler over snug against the foot.

STEP 4

Edge the quilting line into position so it is ¼″ away from the edge of the ruler. You can cut a little ¼″ piece of quilting plastic or paper to help with this.

STEP 5

Holding both the top and bobbin threads, take a few stitches *very* close together to lock the threads.

STEP 6

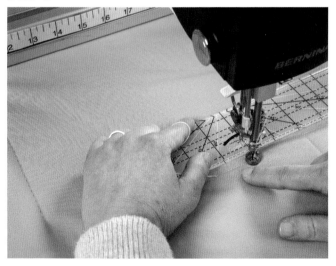

Gradually increase the stitch length so that it *looks* like it is between a 2.5 and 3.0 for a loose or medium design like a straight line or gentle curve, or between a 2.0 and 2.5 for a steeper curve.

STEP 7

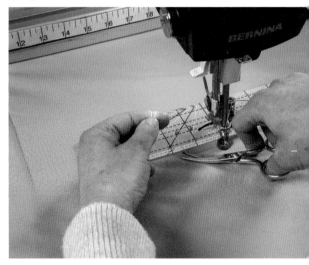

Clip your starting threads right at the quilt sandwich.

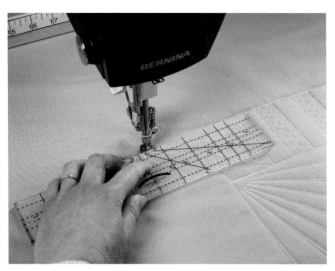

A lot of the time, on a longarm, the position of the ruler is determined for you, because you really can't rotate your quilt top at all! So sometimes you will be holding your ruler in front of the foot ...

... sometimes to the side ...

STEP 8

... and sometimes in back! It's just determined by the shape of your rulers and the design you are trying to create.

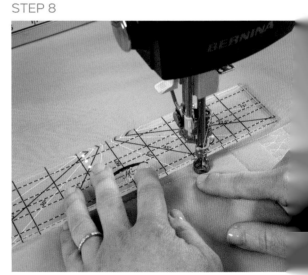

Continue quilting at a normal stitch length until you are ready to end your threads. To do so, quilt a few stitches close together.

↑ Bring up the needle and presser foot.

↑ Grab onto the thread coming out of the needle.

STEP 9

↑ Holding onto this top thread, lower the presser foot and take one more stitch and then raise both the needle and the presser foot. Pull on both the loop of thread that you are holding and the thread coming out of the needle to bring the bobbin thread up through the quilt sandwich.

STEP 10

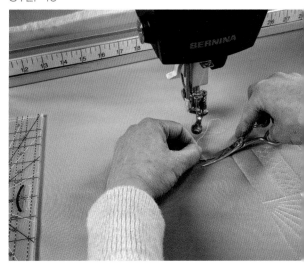

↑ Move the quilt at least 1″ away from its original position and clip the threads at the surface. This will leave the bobbin thread longer and make it easier to bring to the top of the quilt the next time.

Starting and Stopping Threads for Show Quilts

Begin and end your threads for show quilts by leaving your threads long and then later burying them, much as you would on a domestic machine (page 111).

Amanda's Steps for Custom Quilting on a Longarm Machine

Keeping the quilting density uniform throughout ensures a neat and square result.

1. Take a picture of the quilt and make a few copies. Draw with a marker on the copies until you develop a quilting plan that you like.

2. Make sure the backing is square—this is very important! Mount the backing on the longarm.

3. Lay the batting on top. Run a line of basting stitches along the back of the frame, through the backing and batting.

4. Lay the top of the quilt top along the basted line, so that it is square to the frame. Either pin the bottom of the quilt top to the bottom bar or let it float. I personally prefer to let mine float, which means I let it hang off the front of the machine rather than mounting the quilt top on the bottom bar, but I am very careful to keep the quilt square as I roll it. *If you don't want to take any chances, pin the bottom of the quilt to the lower rail at the front of the frame!* If I am going to be working up and down the quilt many times, I mount the backing to the lower front bar in Step 2 and float the top. This keeps the height of the quilt uniform, regardless where I am in the process.

5. Adjust the quilt top so the first seam is parallel to the leveling bar on the back, if needed. Use the seam rather than the quilt top edge, which can be wobbly.

6. Baste around the sides and top of the quilt top, basting as far as you can without rolling the quilt.

7. Clamp the sides of the quilt.

8. Do all the quilting-in-the-ditch that you can reach, along with any other large rulerwork motifs. If desired, you can also do large free-motion work. You must do enough quilting that the fabric won't fold on the bars as you work down the quilt!

9. Unclamp the quilt, roll it, and repeat Steps 6–8 until you finish working down the quilt top.

10. Work back up the quilt, filling in any medium-density free-motion.

11. Work back down the quilt, filling in with stipple or very detailed free-motion.

Ergonomic Tips for Longarm Machines

When you are quilting at a long arm, think about making big movements—almost like you are dancing. Just as with a domestic, the bigger movement will help you keep your shoulders down, and it will be kinder to your wrists!

And, again, take breaks! Set your phone alarm to take a break for a few minutes every hour. Get a glass of water and stretch your shoulders by pulling on the bottom of the chair while straightening your back. Or lean forward while pulling your shoulders back, bracing your arms on the sides of a doorway.

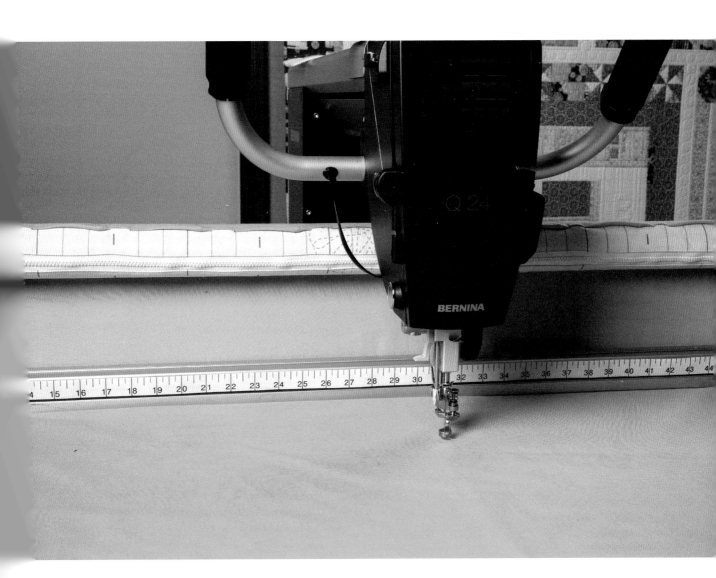

Longarm Rulerwork Troubleshooting

LONGARM PROBLEM 1: MY THREAD TENSION IS OFF.

Possible solutions:

- Your upper thread is not seated properly in the tension discs. Rethread.

- Your bobbin tension is too tight or too loose for the thread you are using. Adjust accordingly.

- Your top tension is too tight or too loose for the thread you are using. Adjust accordingly.

- Your bobbin is seated or wound incorrectly. Try another bobbin.

- You are using a specialty thread that requires a different thread in the bobbin. Consult the manufacturer for their bobbin thread recommendations.

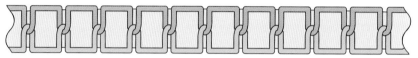

Correct thread tension

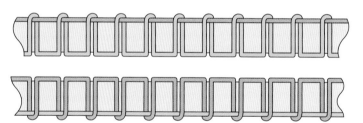

Incorrect thread tension

LONGARM PROBLEM 2: MOST OF MY THREAD TENSION IS GOOD, *BUT* I HAVE PROBLEMS AT THE CORNERS OF MY DESIGNS.

- *Solution:* Quilt two stitches on top of each other at when changing directions. This will lock the threads and make pulled stitches less likely to occur.

LONGARM PROBLEM 3: MY THREAD KEEPS BREAKING *OR*
I'M GETTING SKIPPED STITCHES.

Possible solutions:

- Your machine has too much lint buildup. Treat it to a thorough cleaning.

- Your machine needs oil. (Not all machines take oil—consult your dealer if you have questions.)

- Your needle is not the appropriate size for the thread you are using. Change your needle to a larger size or try a top stitch needle, which has a larger eye.

- There is a burr on your needle or it has gotten dull. Change your needle.

- You might have a bad (or just old!) spool of thread. Switch to another spool and see if the problem continues.

- The dead bar might be at the incorrect height.

LONGARM PROBLEM 4: I AM HAVING DIFFICULTY MOVING
THE MACHINE.

Possible solutions:

- Make sure you're not holding the ruler with a death grip! Loosen up and relax!

- Your dead bar has slipped and is too close to the machine. Adjust its height.

- Make sure the tracks upon which the machine moves are clear and clean.

- Make sure the wheels on the bottom of the machine and the tracks it runs on are clean.

LONGARM PROBLEM 5: MY RULER IS SLIPPING!

Possible solutions:

- Make sure you are holding the ruler firmly enough.

- Make sure you are applying pressure only onto the portion of the ruler backed by the ruler table. (Don't hold the ruler off the table's surface or it might tip!)

- Be sure not to try to quilt too far a distance before you stop and reposition your hands.

- If you are using nested rulers, tape a few together for more surface area (see Help! I Have Nested Circles!, page 41).

LONGARM PROBLEM 6: WHEN I WORK BACK UP MY PIECE AFTER MY FIRST PASS OF QUILTING, THERE ARE FOLDS IN MY QUILT.

- *Solution:* Get more quilting into the quilt before you roll to quilt the next section. Remember, you must have some basic quilting everywhere before you roll.

LONGARM PROBLEM 7: MY QUILT TOP IS NARROWER AT THE BOTTOM THAN IT IS AT THE TOP.

- *Solution:* You've probably floated your quilt top and inadvertently forget to watch that it stays straight. Consider pinning the bottom of the quilt to the lower rail at the front of the frame, instead of letting it hang, until you get more practice and know what to watch for!

Photo by Amanda Murphy

About the Author

Amanda Murphy is a quilt and fabric designer whose style bridges the modern and traditional. She is a BERNINA Expert and Quilting and Longarm Spokesperson, popular teacher, fabric designer for Contempo of Benartex, and pattern designer under her own label. She has designed dozens of quilting and embroidery collections for OESD. In 2018, Amanda designed the fabric, embroidery, and quilt to commemorate BERNINA's 125th anniversary.

Amanda has authored several books with C&T Publishing, including the best-selling *Free-Motion Quilting Idea Book* and *Rulerwork Quilting Idea Book* and most recently *Organic Free-Motion Quilting Idea Book*. Her Good Measure line of quilting rulers is manufactured by Brewer Sewing and features clear markings and a nonslip backing.

Amanda enjoys every part of the quilting process, from designing and choosing fabrics, to integrating piecing and appliqué techniques, to the quilting itself. The best part of her job is seeing people use her fabrics, books, and patterns to create their own works of art!

↑ Photo courtesy of BERNINA of America, Inc.

VISIT AMANDA ONLINE AND FOLLOW ON SOCIAL MEDIA!

Website: blog.amandamurphydesign.com

With links for shop, downloads, and more!

Facebook: /amandamurphyfabrics

Facebook group: Quilting with Amanda Murphy

Pinterest: /amdfabrics

Instagram: @amandamurphydesign

Twitter: @amandarmurphy

YouTube: /amandamurphydesign

ALSO BY AMANDA MURPHY:

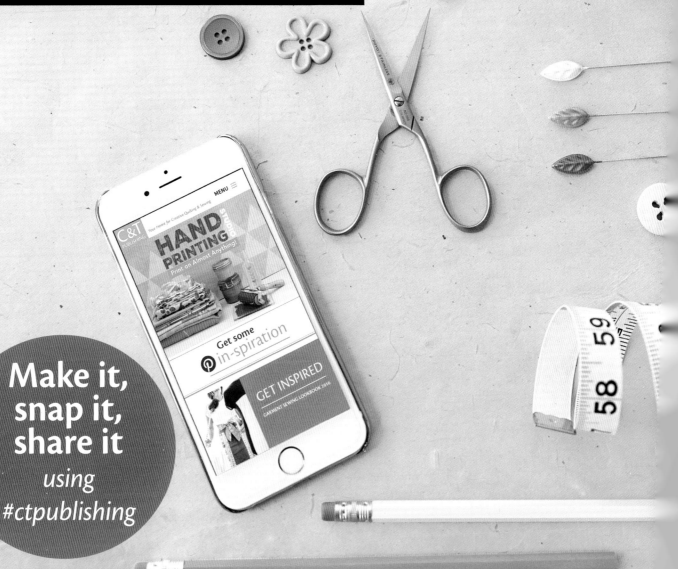

Want even more creative content?

Make it, snap it, share it *using #ctpublishing*